T0363553

ENGAGE

How to engage senior leaders and boards without burning nights and weekends iterating on papers

Davina Stanley

First published in 2024 by Clarity First (US) LLC

© Clarity First (US) LLC

The moral rights of the author have been asserted.

All rights reserved. Except as permitted under the United States *Copyright Act of 1976* (for example, a fair dealing for the purposes of study, research, criticism or review), no part of this book may be reproduced, stored in a retrieval system, communicated or transmitted in any form or by any means without prior written permission.

All inquiries should be made to the author.

ISBN: 978-1-923007-1-54

Project management and text design by Publish Central
Cover design by Pipeline Design

Disclaimer

The material in this publication is of the nature of general comment only, and does not represent professional advice. It is not intended to provide specific guidance for particular circumstances and it should not be relied on as the basis for any decision to take action or not take action on any matter which it covers. Readers should obtain professional advice where appropriate, before making any such decision. To the maximum extent permitted by law, the author and associated entities and publisher disclaim all responsibility and liability to any person, arising directly or indirectly from any person taking or not taking action based on the information in this publication.

I encourage you to unlock the power of clear communication in the boardroom with Engage, *the essential guidebook for executives and board members.*

Drawing on decades of experience working with top-level executives, Davina provides invaluable insights into identifying communication pitfalls with brilliant message mapping strategies.

Whether you're a seasoned CEO or just starting out in the business world, Engage *offers practical strategies for improving communication skills and achieving greater success. Get ready to elevate your communication game and achieve your goals with* Engage.

John Lee, CEO, Work from Anywhere

I prepared my analysis using a message map and my CEO said the leadership team had agreed that it was so clear, they could decide without meeting to discuss.

Charl-Stephan Nienaber, Manager, Strategy and Innovation, Provum Ventures

Davina Stanley really knows what is going on in organisation when it comes to writing: she gives the most realistic description I have ever seen of the 'chain of pain' of having to deal with endless revisions full of Word's 'track changes'.

That means that she, as no other, can offer help to all those struggling writers out there: the book is full of useful instruments that not only speed up the writing process, but also lead to better decision-making.

Louise Cornelis, writing consultant, Netherlands

Contents

Acknowledgements

Many people have helped me write this book – not least the many clients who have let me help with their communication.

Some, however, deserve to be called out as they have been closely involved with this project and its companion book, *Elevate*.

My 'brains trust'. Brendon Jones, Brian Edler, Brooke El Azzi, Clement Armstrong, Mike Sherman, Phil Leacock and Ravi David have been long-time collaborators who have stretched my thinking. Jasmine Parer, Louise Cornelis and Wayne Lewis were also generous with their time and suggestions.

My inspirations. I stand on big shoulders, having begun my career as a communication specialist at McKinsey in Hong Kong, and having access to the ideas of the Firm's greatest communicators. Having my Pyramid Principle training evaluated by Barbara Minto of Pyramid Principle fame also inspired me to push myself harder to master structured communication techniques.

I also very much appreciate smart questions from colleagues such as James Deighton. James years ago presciently asked me questions like, 'But ... how do we get the team to actually do this?' These led me to think about implementing structured thinking from a leadership standpoint, which in turn led to first, *Elevate* for leaders and then this book to complete the set.

My colleagues, past and present. Your enthusiasm and challenge over the years has been invaluable. Sheena, Fatima and Maria, my personal team, you have been indispensable.

My family. My toughest and most valuable critics and my biggest support. Thank you.

Introduction

You are sitting down to review yet another round of comments your manager has sent through on your latest senior leadership team (SLT) paper.

This is the fourth round of minutiae you have received. Ugh.

Minor comments and tweaks have been added using track changes throughout. Many contradict each other. The draft is a sea of red and you can't work out what is wrong.

This is the first key paper you have prepared in this role, so you leveraged examples your predecessor left you. You have also improved on them, thoroughly addressing every topic the required template raises, so this paper should deliver what is needed.

On top of this, you urgently need leadership support to move forward.

But your stakeholders' continual focus on minutiae is driving you nuts. They are muddying the message you work toward at the end of the paper.

What on earth is going on? Seemingly endless rounds of minor edits are getting in the way of a project that will make a real difference to your division's ability to meet its key performance indicators.

And yet, if you don't finalise this paper tomorrow, you will miss the submission date for the next SLT meeting, which will then delay your chance of getting the fast board approval you need.

You settle in for a long night. Your days are 'flat out' moving the project forward, and the last thing you want is for your manager to rewrite your paper again.

Does this sound familiar?

Many executives tell me they regularly redraft papers multiple times, and that it is not uncommon to present to leadership more than once before getting a decision.

They think this is normal.

It comes with the territory.

But ... does it need to?

I don't think so.

I have seen many executives turn this around and look forward to helping you do the same.

Wouldn't it be amazing if you consistently got better, faster decisions from papers and presentations that are (mostly!) written within regular working hours?

This book helps you do that in three parts.

I'll preview them in the coming pages before diving into the details.

▶ Lay foundations

Let's begin at the beginning so you have a strong base to work from. There are many ways to think about communication, so I first want to share mine so you can see how it is distinctive.

Chapter 1. *Think differently about your communication.* In this chapter, I help you discover where opportunities lie and how to set realistic targets for yourself. Whether you have heard of structured thinking before or not, I offer some new ideas to help you think differently about your communication.

Chapter 2. *Iterate early and fast around your top-line messaging.* In this chapter, I offer ideas for lifting the speed and quality of collaboration around key communication. This is central to lifting the quality of messaging that in turn engages decision-makers.

▶ Elevate your structured thinking skills

Now it's time to see how you can change the way you think and work, both on your own and when collaborating. I walk through your role in preparing papers and presentations that will better engage senior leaders. To the right you can see a summary of my Elevate framework, which forms the core of my framework and this book.

Chapter 3. *Flush out your strategy before you write anything.* The biggest mistake I see people make is to dive straight into writing and building beautiful PowerPoint charts without being crystal clear about the desired outcome. I offer a specific technique for clarifying what you want to achieve with each paper or presentation.

Chapter 4. *Frame your message using patterns as a quick start.* In helping thousands of people elevate the quality of their thinking and communication over decades, I have seen patterns emerge in their stories. In this chapter, I demonstrate how you can use my favourites to help you find your message fast.

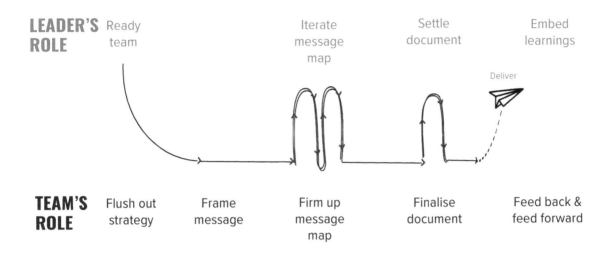

Chapter 5. *Firm up the messaging by iterating around a one-page message map.* Here I explain how you can rely on the structure of your one-page message map to surface and test the quality of your messaging. I dive deeply into 13 key questions you can use to test every aspect of your story.

Chapter 6. *Finalise your document to engage decision-makers.* Once the messaging is firm, translating it into a paper or presentation is relatively easy. I illustrate how to visualise the hierarchy of your messaging so it matches the hierarchy of the formatting in your document.

Chapter 7. *Feed back and feed forward.* A significant missed opportunity arises when you don't take a few moments to reflect on what went well, what didn't and what you can do differently next time. I offer techniques in this chapter for you to do that.

▶ Stay the course

Let's now take these ideas beyond being just that. Here, I encourage you to not just gather a few good ideas, but also put them into practice.

Chapter 8. *Flourish into the long term.* For marginally little effort, you will see the compounding effect of greater velocity achieved from clearer and more insightful communication. I offer some ideas to help you avoid this being a 'flash in the pan' idea, but rather a long-term set of behaviours, habits and expectations.

Chapter 9. *Finish well.* I hope that before you get to this point you will have already used some of the ideas in your work. Here are a few final remarks before I leave you to it.

At each stage, I offer tips, tools and templates developed over more than two decades of practice. As a bonus, you can access editable versions of many of the tools and templates I mention through this book in my online Clarity Hub – ClarityFirstProgram.com/ClarityHub. You also receive one month's free membership to explore the other resources and MasterClasses.

You'll also notice that my headings throughout this book help you skim by encapsulating the key ideas. This is a key benefit that structuring your message brings, and one of the many reasons I have employed the strategy in writing this book.

It's time to get your projects approved – and get your weekends back. Let's get started.

MasterClasses, tools and templates in the Clarity Hub

ClarityFirstProgram.com/ClarityHub

PART I

Lay foundations

CHAPTER 1

Think differently about your communication

Given you are reading this book, I assume you are interested in lifting your communication skills and overall performance. Perhaps you are constantly on the lookout for ways to improve or perhaps your leaders have asked you to focus on this area.

Assuming that strengthening writing or presentation skills might do the trick is tempting. However, in my experience, great writing and powerful presenting do not *cause* great communication. They are the *consequence* of great thinking. This leads to clarity and confidence, which in turn leads to great writing and powerful presenting. I find that when ideas are clear, the writing or the presentation flows much better.

But how do you get your thinking clear in a fast and efficient way? How do you develop and deliver powerful papers and presentations without being stuck iterating around the finer details?

And, particularly, how do you maintain high standards while collaborating in often messy ways with peers and stakeholders?

The trick is to go beyond yourself and your communication output and to look at the ways of working that created that output.

As one of my CEO clients said:

The last thing I want is to polish each paper to perfection by constant iteration. I want a scalable 'system' that I can roll out across the organisation that supports better, faster decision-making.

So, let's lay some strong foundations so you are ready to elevate the quality of your papers and presentations. Here's a preview before we dig into each of these five sections:

▶ Focus more on decisions and less on documents.
▶ Understand why stakeholders rework or reject papers.
▶ Assess your communication against three key metrics.
▶ Be inspired by other people's experience
▶ Get a buddy.

▶ Focus more on decisions and less on documents

While much of this book focuses on papers and presentations, putting these documents in perspective is worthwhile.

Papers and presentations are an important part of decision-making and governance processes; however, they are a means to an end, not an end in themselves.

You may be shocked at the idea of lengthy papers or presentations not being needed to make a decision, but this is exactly what can happen when you make the decisions the focus, rather than the documents.

This idea is captured beautifully by my ex-McKinsey colleague Mike Sherman when we were discussing this book:

My SingTel R&D analytics team worked extensively on the executive summary (my word for the map) and building a tight deck that followed.

When we presented the summary to the division CEO, he responded with, 'Got it, this is a great idea, go ahead with it'.

Amy, the head of the team, spluttered, 'But don't you want to go through the deck?'

To which he replied, 'No. What you propose is clear, the support is clear, the next steps are clear; I have confidence the deck will support what you've just presented, I don't need to see the details'.

This blew her away – but after that she understood that investing time in the executive summary saved so much time down the road.

The three critical messages I want you to take from this are:

1. *Assuming the analysis is accurate, the quality of the high-level messaging is what matters most.* If this is clear and insightful, you will inspire greater confidence in your stakeholders. The clarity and quality of insight show that you have done the work.

2. *This is a team effort.* The opportunity and the challenge are to collaborate to clarify your messaging. Others can see what you miss partly because they are not in the weeds like you are, but also because they bring different perspectives. Your leader in particular can contribute substantively here. You need to bring them into the process early so you and your team deliver maximum impact.

3. *It's both possible and helpful to map complex ideas on a single page.* It is reasonable to be skeptical at this point. You might think your communication is too complex to distill down to a single page. It's true that some complex pieces – such as a book like this– need multiple one-pagers for each section. The high-level messaging can still be (and was!) mapped on a page, however

it may help you to see what Mike is referring to when he talks about a message map or an executive summary.

I offer clients a framework like the one below to help them clarify their messaging. This is the anchor of our process, and I will explain how it works in more depth as we progress.

Now it's time to think more about your stakeholders.

Message map outline

Insert a brief introduction here that explains WHAT you are discussing and WHY you are discussing it with this audience right now.	Single, insightful message that ties your whole paper together		
	Key insight 1	Key insight 2	Key insight 3
	• 2 to 5 supporting points arranged using either a grouping or deductive structure.	• 2 to 5 supporting points arranged using either a grouping or deductive structure.	• 2 to 5 supporting points arranged using either a grouping or deductive structure.

▶ Understand why stakeholders rework or reject papers

Why do managers and other stakeholders so routinely get out their red pen? Why is so much time spent playing 'ping-pong', batting papers to and fro in an attempt to squeeze out the message?

What drives executives to spend their nights and weekends reworking papers rather than getting the fast decisions they need? Here are four issues I see driving this:

▶ Insights are too hard to find.

▶ Iteration relies on Track Changes.

▶ Teams prepare papers with little understanding of the desired outcome.

▶ Leaders leave their contribution to the last minute.

Insights are too hard to find

In my experience, problems with papers and presentations rarely result from an ability to use words or to craft sentences. Even if you are not working in your first language, you no doubt perform at a fairly high level in your work. You couldn't do what you do if you weren't at least moderately proficient in the language.

The big question is why decent language ability is not sufficient to craft papers that engage decision-makers.

After all, when we read someone's communication, words and sentences are *what we see.*

We first see poor language use and any obvious typographical errors. These lead us to worry that the insights aren't there because *we can't find them.*

To help you think about whether this is an issue in your communication, see if any of these four problems resonate with you:

▶ *The wafer:* Ideas are loosely connected and light on detail. The paper does not provide sufficient detail to be convincing.

▶ *The Easter egg hunt:* Insights are buried in a slew of facts, some relevant, some not. This forces the reader to hunt for the insights.

▶ *The Agatha Christie:* Insights are saved for the end, requiring the reader to work their way through your thinking process before the big reveal.

▶ *The miss:* You have a potentially strong narrative but have addressed the wrong issues, even if those covered are technically accurate.

Think about the most recent papers you have prepared. Did any of these problems arise?

Iteration relies on Track Changes

I wonder if you dislike Track Changes as much as I do? Although this is a wonderfully useful tool at the right time, iterating around Track Changes too early creates a hot mess.

Passing a draft from person to person who each adds comments or tweaks using Track Changes keeps everyone iterating in the weeds. It also leads to many (many) unnecessary iterations, full of comments that focus on minutiae.

Below shows an example of the sorts of comments I see alongside documents edited this way. You can see they focus on fine detail rather than the bigger picture messaging.

Ask yourself, how many versions does this process typically require before landing the final one?

Although this is a little extreme, I have seen clients draft 60+ versions of 10-page papers before landing their final version. More commonly, I see five to 10 iterations. Either way, the time sink is unbelievable in relation to the gains.

~~Track Changes keeps everyone in the weeds~~

 Mary
Will need to provide a couple of examples.

 Fred
Lovely word, but jargon?

 Mary
This needs some context. eg – while this work is via multiple initiatives, this is not reflected and tracked as HRIs in the RIS.

 Mary
Which time? Think Kylie mentioning the 3Q20 deadline to operationalise?

 Fred
Bit contradictory. First line says significant work is performed vs significant work remains.

 Mary
Bit abrupt?

I have also had workshop participants yelp when they realise *why* their papers were rejected multiple times. In one instance, a group of mining engineers realised their paper was repeatedly rejected because it answered the wrong question. No matter how beautifully they wrote that paper, it was never going to land until that question 'clicked'. It was a 'miss'.

In all these situations, the teams used a variation of a process I call the Chain of Pain.

I have yet to work with a team who doesn't either groan or laugh in embarrassment when I show them the Chain of Pain diagram below. Here's how it works:

1. Someone requests a paper.
2. Someone writes a draft, most likely going to some trouble to make the prose elegant and the charts better than just presentable.
3. They then send the draft around to other peers and stakeholders for their input. Here leaders focus on minutiae because they can't see the big picture. They make comments such as (and I quote), 'bit contradictory', 'bit vague', 'lovely word but the manager would call that jargon'.
4. Eventually the author gets the paper back, fixes typos and sends it to their manager for review, with little sense of ownership of the message or the document.

Do you experience the Chain of Pain?

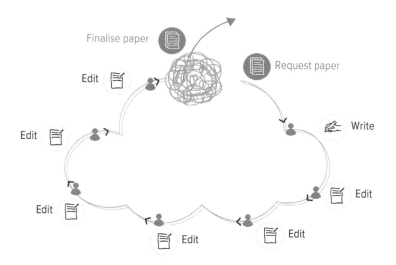

If you're the author, the paper is sent back to you to review and adopt the mish mash of changes. This can leave you with a huge challenge as you attempt to understand and evaluate each person's contributions ... and then decide what to do with them.

Regardless of your decisions, the document rarely ends up delivering a cohesive narrative after a Chain of Pain has taken place.

Teams prepare papers with little understanding of the desired outcome

When I work with teams, I ask some benchmarking questions at the start of the process and compare their answers against those questions at the end of our time together.

One element I focus on is a team's view of the quality of the briefings they receive before preparing papers.

Shifting the results depends on both leaders and paper writers working together at the start of the process. As we go further in this book, I will explain this more deeply, but for now I want to highlight the importance of clarifying the desired outcome for that paper from the start.

Think about how much time you spend guessing what should be included in papers and reworking them. What if you could cut that time by about a third?

My data suggests that is imminently doable and possibly conservative. You may well be able to halve the total time sink – while also providing greater clarity, higher quality insights and greater working velocity.

Leaders leave their contribution until the last minute

You might wonder why papers are so often finalised under pressure, even if the early drafts are prepared well ahead of time.

When the key insights are hard to find, managers and other stakeholders often delay making their contribution.

They take a quick look at a draft, realise it needs more than a quick review, and so 'park it' until they have time to focus properly on the details. They need thinking time that doesn't come easily.

As a result, the paper lingers until it becomes urgent. This then leaves managers in a quandary. How do they proceed when the paper clearly misses the mark? They will be treading on the author's toes if they rework it and yet it isn't fit for purpose.

Do they 'let it go' and punt that their voiceover will suffice, rework it together with the author, or just redo in private and hope the revised example will provide a guide for next time? The image above sums up this process.

If the leader decides to dig into it on their own, their natural instinct is to tinker with the details to create order so they can see what it is all about. In other words, they start doing the thinking work for you.

Where to now?

▶ Assess your communication against three key metrics

Where do you want to get to? What is realistic? How aspirational are you?

My hunch is that the single most important needle to move is the amount of time you spend reworking important papers. If you spend less time reworking them, you may be confident your communication is improving.

That single measure may be enough. You may, however, like to dig deeper to know what leaders are looking for.

Here are the three dimensions that I use to think about communication quality:

1. *Clarity:* Can you glean the core messages within 30 seconds of opening a paper or presentation?
2. *Quality:* How valuable are the insights?
3. *Velocity:* How quickly can you clarify and convey powerful insights that lead to better decisions?

Let's now look at these in line with specific client stories to bring them to life.

Clarity: Can you glean the core messages within 30 seconds?

It helps to ask how easily the insights jump off the page so your audience can grasp them quickly. How easy are they to find in the paper, presentation, discussion, email or other communication form?

One board director summed up what she wants. She loathes the feeling that comes when opening a paper or presentation to find an impenetrable wall of text. the instant realisation that undersanding the paper will be hard can be visceral.

Instead, she wants messages to pop off the page so she can skim before deciding how to read deeply.

How often can your audience glean the message within 30 seconds of opening a paper, presentation or email of yours?

While clarity is critical, it's not enough. To quote one of my 'crustier' clients, the head of credit risk at a large bank:

The team can now craft much clearer communication, which is great. But how do we stop them putting 'rubbish' in the boxes?

This leads me to my next dimension: quality of insight.

Quality: How valuable are the insights?

Do your papers deliver significant value to the project, team or organisation? Do they connect some dots to offer a new idea that adds value to the strategy, or perhaps reduce risk?

This is where both the challenge and the opportunity lie.

In *A Whole New Mind*, best-selling author Daniel Pink argues synthesis is the 'killer app' in business in what he calls the new Conceptual Age. Pink highlights:

What's in greatest demand today isn't analysis but synthesis – seeing the big picture and crossing boundaries, being able to combine disparate pieces into an arresting new whole.

Or, more simply, the formula we used at McKinsey:

SYNTHESIS = SUMMARY + INSIGHT

Daniel Pink is right. Most people can summarise – but so can natural language processing tools such as ChatGPT, if given the right data set.

The real value we humans bring is to join the facts with our own insights about the organisational context.

So, to offer high-quality, valuable insights, a team needs to be technically strong and in touch with the commercial and stakeholder imperatives.

This means adopting a common strategy for tying together complex ideas to make them *seem simple*.

This brings me to my third ingredient: velocity.

Velocity: How quickly can your team clarify and convey powerful insights that drive quality decisions?

Colin Bryar and Bill Carr were members of Amazon's senior leadership team. Their excellent book *Working Backwards*, which describes Amazon's secret to success, provides many insights.

The principle of velocity was one of them.

Amazon has gone to great lengths to maintain velocity in all areas of its operations so it can continue to execute quickly on innovative business lines. Removing bottlenecks is central.

Thinking like this about the processes surrounding your major communication deliverables will also help you.

Imagine if your board paper received 'minimal adjustments' at each layer of your organisation's approval chain. Even better,

imagine the board approving the idea the first time it is presented.

A client from the supply chain team at a large retailer coined a term to describe this: the Gold Standard. Here's how it works.

An individual or a team prepares a one-page message map before socialising that page with stakeholders. This one-pager triggers constructive debate around the big-picture ideas and how they connect with the data.

By socialising this message map rather than a polished document, at least three important things happen:

1. Everyone can review the message map and respond quickly with constructive suggestions to refine the thinking. One CEO client tells me he spends about 15 minutes reviewing each one-pager before the team prepares the final paper or presentation. This is a fraction of the time he previously spent reviewing papers for the senior leadership team and the board.

2. Stakeholders are more willing and able to debate the ideas. When someone receives a full document that someone has obviously 'sweated over', they feel less comfortable having the debate. Doing so feels more like a 'correction' than a 'conversation'.

3. The team spends less time preparing prose and charts that not only turn out to be off point, but which are also hard to let go of. As soon as someone creates a chart or writes a section, they can find it hard to let go. They spend time trying to 'fit it in' rather than stepping back and looking at the overall message they need to convey.

4. You spend more energy thinking about the issues that matter, rather than wading through micro comments and changes.

All of this liberates you from the awful game of 'red pen ping-pong' so you can focus on higher order activities.

My clients frequently see a 30 per cent lift in velocity when drafting papers and presentations. This impacts both team members and leaders. Some teams, such as those outlined in the next section, achieve materially more than that.

▶ Be inspired by other people's experience

I have hundreds and hundreds of stories I could share but in this section I have chosen three that I hope will resonate with you.

I suggest reading them and then imagining what you would like to say about your own achievements after implementing the ideas in this book.

Project management office cut prep time by 80 per cent

One client was a project management office (PMO) in a large company. They shredded their preparation time for papers and presentations by 80 per cent, while simultaneously consistently getting decisions after 15 minutes. Let me unpack that for you:

▶ *Before:* They spent about 15 hours across the team to prepare for each steering committee meeting. These meetings frequently took two to three hours and led to more questions rather than decisions.

▶ *After:* Once they changed their preparation process, they took two to three hours to finalise their messaging. This then led to a 15-minute discussion that reliably led to a concrete decision.

Safety review cut from two hours to eight minutes

In another instance, a head of safety for a retailer changed the dynamic for his quarterly updates with the CFO. These meetings went from two hours of him answering clarification questions about his 60-page presentation deck, to two questions that he was able to answer in eight minutes.

He and the CFO then enjoyed a quality discussion around the safety status and strategy, rather than unpicking the detail of the past quarter's slips and trips.

Analyst report led to senior leadership team meeting cancellation

A strategy analyst for a retirement village company had investigated the key drivers of poor performance in the company, and now needed to report his findings to the leadership. He sent an email outlining his high-level messaging and attached a detailed PowerPoint explaining the performance drivers.

The PowerPoint reiterated the high-level messages and supported each one with detailed evidence.

He received a thank you email from the CEO who said, 'You have laid out the situation so clearly, we don't need to meet to discuss this. We can see what we need to do'.

This meant six senior people each spent less time understanding the findings, and each got half an hour back from a cancelled meeting. It also put my client, who was new to his role, in a positive light with people several levels above him in the organisation.

You can achieve these kinds of results too. And it all happens much faster if you learn with someone else.

▶ Get a buddy

One of my favourite buddy stories comes from teaching lawyers. I worked for a large firm for five years. Over a year my colleague and I visited every office to ensure all new hires received training and incumbents received support. This meant that one small office received only one visit each year.

Two new senior associates joined this office soon after my visit one year and so took the matter into their own hands. They realised they needed to catch up with this new way of writing letters of advice, which were core to their work.

Their solution was to ask a colleague to run them through the approach, borrow their learning journal from my program and then commit to collaborate when creating a one-page message map for every key communication for a month.

Given they billed their time in six-minute units, they expected to be working very long days to help each other learn this new way while simultaneously meeting their billings targets.

However, they were surprised to find that they did not take a hit to their billable hours.

By working together, they saved time and created better quality advice.

So, I encourage you to find a buddy to work alongside you. You can decide whether this is someone at work, or a past colleague. It doesn't matter. Having someone to ask how you are progressing, and to share your challenges and successes with will keep you moving forward.

You will not only magnify the benefits for yourself, but also strengthen your relationships with a colleague (or two!).

Now I've hopefully engaged you in the idea of surfacing your messaging on a highly structured one-pager, it's time to think about how to focus your collaboration around it.

CHAPTER 2

Iterate quickly and early around the top-line messaging

I have talked so far about the importance of focusing on the high-level messaging.

My Elevate framework (below) helps you collaborate effectively to deliver higher quality communication more quickly.

It gets the best out of you and your colleagues' knowledge and experience quick time. It helps you combine your own knowledge with your colleagues' situational awareness, influence skills, business acumen and domain knowledge at the start.

This adds rocket fuel to your ability to quickly prepare high-quality communication.

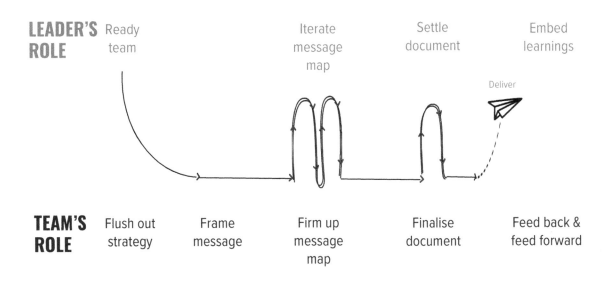

Even if working solo, you can still take great strides. I am yet to meet a leader who does not value their team members making the effort.

I will now preview how you can iterate fast and early around your messaging in collaboration with your colleagues and leaders. I explain the importance of each step before then diving more deeply into how each one works.

I explain why it helps to:

▶ Flush out the communication strategy before writing anything.

▶ Frame the messaging using patterns as a quick-start.

▶ Firm up messaging by quickly iterating around a one-page message map.

▶ Finalise the document so it engages decision-makers.

▶ Feed back and feed forward to embed learnings from all involved.

I'll now dig into why each of these steps matters.

▶ Flush out the communication strategy before writing anything

Every executive I have worked with has at some point commented on how much time it can take to work out what is required from key papers. The distance between the author and the audience can be vast, and bridging that gap feels like a dark art.

The challenge, however, has much more to do with process than with any sort of 'dark art'. Instead of trying to work out what is required on your own, or with colleagues who are equally in the dark,

I encourage you to get a clear briefing from the person who has requested the paper.

I understand this isn't always easy, so I offer concrete strategies to help in the coming chapter.

For now, I want you to focus on how much faster and easier it is to prepare your papers when you understand who they are *really* for and what they *really* need to achieve.

▶ Frame the messaging using patterns as a quick-start

If you are familiar with design thinking, this technique for prototyping your story might not seem so strange. If not, then sit tight: you will enjoy it!

I have identified 10 common story patterns that suit complex senior stories. These jump-start your thinking, removing the need for you and the team to start from a blank page. I'll now explain how these patterns help you. They:

▶ Support a wide range of situations

▶ Help prototype your message so it 'clicks' early

▶ Offer flexibility within a framework.

I'll now expand on each of these to explain further.

Patterns support a wide range of situations

I have been experimenting with patterns for many years to help my clients clarify their thinking faster.[1] It seems to be easier to react to something than start from scratch and so I have codified the commonalities between the thousands of papers I have helped clients prepare.

The 10 patterns I am about to share result from that experimentation. I've found this set to be well suited to structuring communication for senior leaders and boards.

You will notice as I lay them out on the coming two pages that these patterns are heavily weighted toward persuasion.

I find that in many instances where clients assume their audience 'just needs to know', they are missing something. This is especially so for updates. I always dig more deeply to ask why they need to know and, in doing so, frequently unearth the real need. I encourage you to do the same.

Patterns help prototype your message so it 'clicks' early

Given you no longer need to start with a blank sheet, I encourage you to think through your strategy and then prototype – or hack – what your messaging might look like against a couple of promising patterns. In playing with a couple of examples – potentially more than a couple if your thinking is still unclear – you can quickly stress test your messaging.

---

1   Gerard Castles and I published seven useful patterns in our book *The So What Strategy* in 2017.

For informing when little persuasion is needed: Nike and Nugget

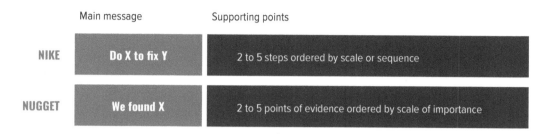

	Main message	Supporting points
NIKE	Do X to fix Y	2 to 5 steps ordered by scale or sequence
NUGGET	We found X	2 to 5 points of evidence ordered by scale of importance

For gaining or maintaining trust when ... 'all is well'!

ALL IS WELL	We are in good shape	2 to 5 reasons why we are in good shape, ordered by task or time

For delivering strategies: Golden, Make the Case and Oh Dear

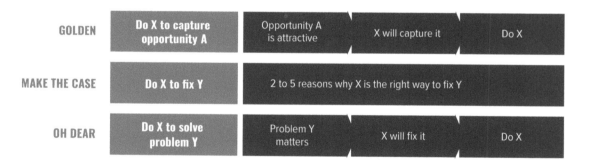

GOLDEN	Do X to capture opportunity A	Opportunity A is attractive	X will capture it	Do X
MAKE THE CASE	Do X to fix Y	2 to 5 reasons why X is the right way to fix Y		
OH DEAR	Do X to solve problem Y	Problem Y matters	X will fix it	Do X

For discussing options: Short List or This or That

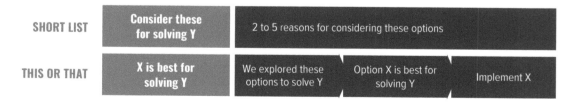

SHORT LIST	Consider these for solving Y	2 to 5 reasons for considering these options		
THIS OR THAT	X is best for solving Y	We explored these options to solve Y	Option X is best for solving Y	Implement X

For recommending improvements: Change Tack or Top Up

Interestingly, I have found that doing this also helps firm up the strategic direction. When looking at a skeleton for a story, you can't always articulate what is working or not; but, you often know that something either is or is not right. This insight nudges you to think harder about what is really needed.

Laying skeletons out against each other is a fast and effective way to tighten the strategy, frame up the story and reduce the risk of preparing whole papers or presentations that must be rewritten – or, worse, whole papers or presentations that are written and then rejected because they miss the point.

You may also find my Pattern Picker a useful adjunct to this process. It guides you through a decision tree to identify promising patterns. I include a simple version in this book and a more nuanced version leading to more sophisticated patterns inside the Clarity Hub[2].

Whichever strategy you use, hold back on preparing the document until you are comfortable with the message. Junking pages and pages of elegant PowerPoint is hard, even when they no longer have a place in the story. So let's reduce the chance that you and your team prepares them in the first place.

Patterns offer flexibility within a framework

I've found patterns to be a terrific way to take advantage of structured thinking techniques without being 'expert'.

By starting with a pattern, you can fairly quickly work out what you need to say. You can then check your draft against structured thinking principles to tighten your thinking. I have three caveats, however.

---

2   ClarityFirstProgram.com/ClarityHub

Firstly, you will most likely quickly find your favourites, and not need to master all 10 patterns.

Secondly, 'tweaking' the structures is risky if you deviate from first principles. These patterns work because they adhere to relatively simple yet important rules of logic and synthesis.

Thirdly, although these are powerful short cuts that cover many situations, they may not be the only structures you ever use.

Once you understand the underlying principles, you can tweak the patterns to better suit your own needs. Sometimes this means merging various aspects of them or flipping them to the opposite direction.

For example, you might notice that the Oh Dear and Golden patterns below are similar. Oh Dear starts introducing a new material problem whereas Golden begins with an attractive opportunity.

In creating these two variants, I 'flipped' the first point (the statement) from the classic negative Oh Dear beginning to a positive, to explain that we have a golden opportunity. With practice, you will be able to do the same.

You can also short cut this process by using the Pattern Picker, which I'll introduce shortly or by using the more nuanced version from the Clarity Hub[3], when your situation is murkier than usual.

Once you have chosen a pattern and fleshed it out as a one-pager, it is time to be confident your messaging is robust.

---

3   ClarityFirstProgram.com/ClarityHub

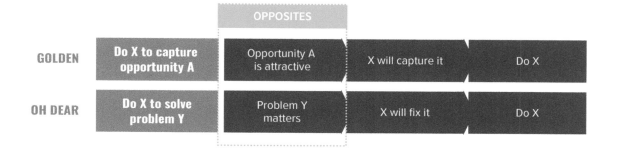

▶ Firm up the messaging by iterating around a one-page message map

This is where structured thinking techniques come into their own in helping you clarify your messaging.

You will first review the messaging yourself using the tests I offer, and then ask a peer to review it before sending it to your manager for their approval. This is the engine-room of my approach. Once this messaging is clear, everything else falls into place.

Reviewing the one-pager is an effective way to offer substantive input and much faster than reviewing a whole paper or presentation.

Understanding how message maps work from structured thinking principles helps you optimise this process to draw out the insights from your information when finalising the full document.

Before we get to the depths of structuring, I'll first explain how message maps help you. They are more than your average template. They:

- ▶ Focus everyone on your main message.
- ▶ Push you to think harder by visualising your ideas into a tight one-pager.
- ▶ Help clarify *and* convey your message.

Let's now explore each of these more fully.

Message maps focus everyone on your main message

As a CEO from an Australian retailer said early on in our working relationship:

Do you mean that I can ask everyone to prepare their one-pagers a week before the SLT or board meeting and then just spend 15 minutes reviewing each one?

I can block off a couple of hours and go through them one by one and pass back my feedback that quickly?

Once he saw how this worked, he mandated that all drafts be sent to him for review in message map format a week before the paper was to be submitted. He is not alone in that recommendation. This enabled him to quickly review the messaging and provide substantive feedback. It was also a fast and effective way to occasionally re-review where major change was needed.

I'll now explain how message maps work alongside a high-level structure before I dive into the details.

Message maps offer a structured way to draw attention to your core message in three parts, each of which has a distinct role to play. The three parts are as follows:

1. A short introduction that is less than 15 per cent of the whole document. Board members and other senior leaders commonly complain that they dislike reading screeds of background at the start of a paper, so keep this short.
2. One single, short message that synthesises the entire message. If your audience only reads one sentence, this is it. It offers a snapshot of the whole paper.
3. Two to five supporting points that are organised logically, using one of two high-level thinking structures. Both rely on logic and synthesis to draw out the messages, so they are easy to convey.

The illustration below shows you how you can map your ideas visually. This helps you focus on the relationships between the ideas, rather than getting lost in screeds of prose or PowerPoint pages.

Understanding the mechanics of each part helps you think through your own messaging and support your team in developing the overall approach. You can do this by working from the detail up or or by leveraging patterns.

Working visually to understand the relationships between the ideas within this message map is key.

Message maps push you to think harder by visualising your ideas as a tight one-pager

Message maps are quite different from a document 'format' or 'template' that offers a list of topics to discuss. The map helps draw out the message from your material

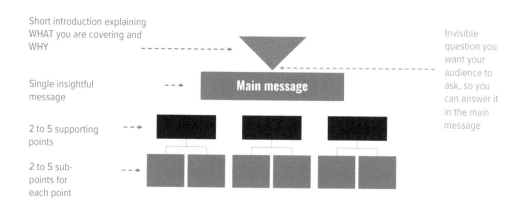

Short introduction explaining WHAT you are covering and WHY

Single insightful message

Main message

Invisible question you want your audience to ask, so you can answer it in the main message

2 to 5 supporting points

2 to 5 sub-points for each point

rather than offering 'buckets' to throw ideas in.

As one of my McKinsey colleagues from years ago said:

A one-pager is a bit like an insight engine. The rules that underpin the structure help us tease out the message.

Whether preparing a high-stakes email that runs to half a page or a book like this one, you can use your one-pager to visualise the relationships between your ideas before preparing your communication. This means that even for a lengthy communication, you have a single A4 (or letter) page with your high-level thinking. For something as long as this book, I then add sub-pages for each chapter that allow me to order the large number of ideas in the levels below.

I don't, however, do what one of my engineering clients did. I had offered this group an introductory workshop and then went to work with them again in more depth. At the start of the session, I asked what they remembered from the introductory session and this was their response:

You said to map our ideas onto a one-pager. We have been really good at doing that. We just decided that A4 was too small, so we went to A1 paper and used 4-point font.

This made me laugh, and I did think it was a fabulous solution – but one that missed the point entirely!

By limiting yourself to working on one small sheet of paper with a minimum of 10-point font, you're forced to summarise and synthesise.

You can 'cover everything' at a high level, but not include every little detail. You also can't include *how we got there* but are required to think hard about what you need to say to get what you need from your audience.

Simply getting 'everything onto a single small page', however, is not enough. In isolation, that will leave you iterating again and again to slowly rise above the detail to find a smaller number of words to share. This smaller number of words usually still requires your decision-makers to read from the beginning to the end to work out what you actually mean.

Instead, you want to use a structured approach to thinking through the issues so you can distil and deliver powerful insights clearly and quickly.

Message maps help clarify *and* convey your message

On the next page I show what a message map looks like for a fairly complex recommendation.

You can see the blue panel on the left offers a brief introduction, with one single overarching message and then three supporting points on the right. Each of those points has a small number of high-level supports also.

This example uses the Oh Dear pattern, which we will revisit during the book. Take the time to read it now to become familiar with the story before seeing it unfold in coming chapters.

Now is also a good time to download a blank message map along with the other slides in my PowerPoint planner from the Clarity Hub Toolkit.[4]

Now I have introduced the basics, let's discuss how to use these one-pagers to create a paper or presentation.

▶ Finalise the document so it engages decision-makers

Once the message map has been locked down, you will prepare the paper or presentation.

The key is to maintain the integrity of the messaging. The more settled the message map is before you turn it into a document, the easier this will be. If it's not fully settled, your ideas will evolve further inside the document, muddying the message.

Knowing when to swap from working inside a message map to working in the document is a bit of an art. Although experience is the best tutor, the longer you wait the easier the transition will be.

Naturally, the more complex the paper and the stakeholder group, the harder it is to get this right. So, I encourage you to first focus on shorter, lower risk communication while not ignoring the opportunity to tackle a good challenge.

Either way, do your best to match the hierarchy of the messaging in the map with the hierarchy of the messaging in the final paper.

This will also make things easier for whoever presents it. The structure of the messaging will be crystal clear for everyone.

---

4   ClarityFirstProgram.com/ClarityHub

Example message map for reference

Meeting regulatory requirements requires us to transition all 105 legacy reports into the case system by the end of this financial year. We have now reviewed the associated work plans and received updated estimates.

We are now ready to share those estimates with you along with potential ways forward.

What are you suggesting?

Delivering the 105 reports means either investing $1.2m to $2m more over the coming two years or renegotiating requirements with the regulator.

Despite stress testing all budgets, we can't transition all 105 regulatory reports within the agreed $2m budget this financial year.	This means we need to make trade-offs when finalising the project workplans.	Therefore, we ask you to advise which tradeoffs we can make.
Updated estimates for database came back at $2m, which is 2.5 x the original budget due to more comprehensive scoping.	**We could meet the scope by spending $1.2m to $2m more over the coming two years.**	**Decide whether to spend more ...**
	• We could deliver everything in FY23 with $1.2m more during FY23, or	• Decide whether to increase funding by $1.2m for FY23.
Budgets for other aspects of the work have not materially changed.	• We could deliver some in FY23, some in FY24 with $2m or more in total.	• Decide whether to budget $2m more for the project in total and roll into next year.
• Workflow remains same.		
• API linking ditto.		**Decide whether to renegotiate ...**
• Operational teams ditto.	**We could renegotiate scope or time with the regulator.**	• Decide whether to pitch the regulator to accept the top 70 reports as adequate for FY23.
Work required for reports identified since June last year has not been factored in.	• We could limit the scope and deliver only the top 70 reports by FY23 (fix existing 36, do another 35ish) within the current budget, or	• Decide whether to seek extensions.
	• We could seek agreement from the regulator to further extend the project and deliver all at a later date.	

▶ Feed back and feed forward to embed the learnings

This is the easiest step to ignore but I can't stress its importance enough. If you want to write papers your leaders can approve without adjustment, you need to hear what worked and what didn't.

You may not be in the steering committee or board meeting and so miss valuable insights. Being part of the meeting helps; however, even that isn't sufficient.

You may not catch all the nuances in the conversation or the stakeholder subtleties, given you most likely have little direct contact with these stakeholders outside this meeting. So follow up with your leaders so you can make adjustments for next time.

You will likely need to ask your manager for their input in your next one-on-one meeting. The pace of business is so fast it's easy to forget to have this conversation.

Now it's time to dig more deeply into these steps, one by one in the coming chapters.

PART II

Elevate your structured thinking skills

CHAPTER 3

Flush out your communication strategy before writing anything

Now you have the general idea, let's get to the meat and potatoes. The first task is to flush out the communication strategy for your paper or presentation before you write anything.

This will help you and your leaders gain extreme clarity around what the communication must achieve, and who the decision-makers really are. This clarity will go a long way to lift the quality of the communication and the effort you all expend to create it.

You will need to work with your colleagues and your leadership to get the information you need to prepare a quality paper.

Here are the four steps to take:

▶ Think about who to involve.

▶ Clarify your desired outcome.

▶ Understand your audience.

▶ Iterate to refine your communication strategy.

I share examples throughout to bring the approach to life, beginning with simpler and more general ones. I do this to introduce the concepts simply first, to reduce the risk that a complex example will get in the way of your conceptual understanding

You will soon see that although the concepts are quite simple, they require you to practise so you squeeze out the very last drop of insight from your material.

▶ Think about who to involve

I mentioned earlier that one challenge with preparing important communication is that leaders often leave their contributions until too late. As someone preparing the paper, this makes your life challenging, and puts you at risk of investing hours – and potentially days – trying to work out who a paper or presentation is for and why they need it. While I realise some of this can be hard to avoid, I offer ideas here to minimise that risk.

The first step is to think about who to involve and what role they might play in preparing the communication. If possible, you can ask for a meeting to flush out the strategy with your manager. If that is not possible, you may need to gather the necessary information from your stakeholders one by one and stress-test it with your manager as soon as you can. Let's look at the best-case situation and you can work back from there.

I recommend involving everyone who will have a role in preparing the paper, including more junior team members who may only focus on discrete sections. You may enjoy the value young, fresh eyes can bring along with some 'smart-dumb' questions. You may also think expansively to include people with the five Es:

- ▶ *Effort:* Do they have sufficient capacity or interest to contribute right now?
- ▶ *Elevation:* Do they have sufficient visibility of the strategic environment to help link your narrative to the broader business objectives?
  You may bring sufficient visibility on your own, or equally, you may bring someone senior into the session to share their perspective.

It could be the person who commissioned the paper, someone who owns the relevant business strategy or someone who knows the stakeholder group well.

- ▶ *Evaluative ability:* Do they bring fresh eyes and raw intelligence that may help the team think from first principles?
- ▶ *Experience:* Do they bring practical, hard-earned wisdom?
- ▶ *Expertise:* Are they familiar with the problem or have a usefully different perspective? Most likely they will have been working on the issue. In gaining a full set of perspectives, you will increase the chances of setting yourself up to deliver a draft message map that hits the right notes.

As an example of how beneficial this process can be, I recently worked with a group of analysts from an energy company. They were astounded at how this briefing lit a match under their ability to develop their messaging. At the end of their one-hour planning session for a business case that resulted from two years of analysis and research, the team had a message map that their leader approved without adjustment.

They then divided up the work of preparing their PowerPoint up section by section and created it quickly.

They were delighted to tell me that their (big) proposal was accepted with only about 10 minutes discussion at the SLT meeting. The SLT was persuaded by the pre-read and had very few questions.

▶ Clarify your desired outcome

Understanding the commercial reality behind a paper and being crystal clear about the associated outcome is central to you and your colleagues performing at the right level.

The first step is to get everyone clear on the desired outcome for the communication. I'll now explain the approach before illustrating with an example.

Approach: Use a tightly structured statement to gain extreme clarity around your desired outcome

This is where much of the deep thinking takes place. In my coaching sessions, the message map comes together quite quickly after the initial thinking about the outcome and the audience is clear. Gaining that clarity can be a bit like peeling an onion, though, where you need to layer into the real situation and the real goal.

This single sentence frames the thinking about what will go into the communication. This statement is not included in the document itself, but used to frame the thinking that does go into the document.

I encourage you to be highly specific when completing the following statement:

> As a result of this **specific piece of communication** *[name it]* I want **my audience** *[name the top person or perhaps top three people who will be pivotal to the decision and/or could derail the implementation]* to **know**, **think** or **do** ... *[name the action you want your audience to take; for example, 'agree', 'decide' or 'understand'].*

Pushing for extreme clarity around the three bold variables turns light bulbs on. You and your colleagues need to drill deeply into which piece of communication you are referring to, which audience member will have the most sway over the decision and what specific outcome you need.

You may be surprised how valuable it is to iterate around this seemingly simple sentence to get away from being general, and therefore fairly meaningless. The more specific you are, the more helpful this statement will be. I'll now illustrate how this works by working through a paper seeking leadership support for a challenging regulatory project.

Example: Re-scoping a derailed project

I chose this example because it is so delightfully real. Tightly designed scopes for well-understood and clearly defined tasks supported by aligned stakeholder groups teach us less. So in this example, I highlight how you can use these concepts in (hopefully relatably) messy situations.

The 'fix these reports now' project was about meeting a regulator's requirement that a bank improve the quality of 105 customer reports. These reports needed to accurately reflect the viability of customer accounts that had changed since their inception.

Customers might have, for example, swapped from one type of loan to another or added more loans or credit cards. These changes alter their aggregate position with the bank. The team needed to deliver better operational workflows, more efficient case

management and more accurate reporting on the status of these customer accounts. This in turn gave greater clarity about the bank's overall financial position.

The project had not made good progress over the year before my client was brought in as manager. He was asked to 'fix it' with $2 million. Success, at a minimum, would be replacing the 105 legacy reports with functioning, automated reports that enabled the bank to know if customer accounts were profitable or not with significantly less manual processing.

His first task was to review the current status before making a recommendation to leadership. He found that despite $3 million being spent over the past year, the team had produced only 33 *unusable* reports. The reports did not, for example, factor in duplicates. This led to overstating problems by up to 70 per cent.

So, my client had a condensed time frame to deliver 105 *usable* reports. To add to the challenge, the IT team had been unavailable over his first three months in the role.

In thinking through your desired outcome and audience for a paper like this, you might focus on leaders with the most interest in and influence over this project. This will likely be gleaned from experience, your understanding of each member's roles and responsibilities, their past behaviour when budgets are challenged and what they have said about the topic in previous meetings.

In that case, your statement might be something like this:

> As a result of this **paper**, I want the **executive** to **approve another $1.2 million in funding so we can complete the 105 reports on time at the end of this financial year**.

This draft offers a useful starting point. You will see, though, that as the audience is better understood, it can be finessed further to be more accurate and more useful.

This draft initially felt like the right ask given the project manager's understanding of the looming 'mortgage cliff'. A large number of home loans would soon expire, leading borrowers to renegotiate at a likely higher and unaffordable rate.

His view was that the project needed more money and focus to reduce the impact of significant interest rate hikes that would lead borrowers to change their loans. These changes would then need to be manually updated in the current legacy reports that help the bank understand its position … unless the project succeeded in updating the reports ASAP.

As you will soon see, his view morphed as together we better understood the audience. This revised view was then reflected in a revised outcome statement.

▶ Understand your audience deeply

Once you have identified who the most influential stakeholders will be, unpacking their mindset around your topic can be helpful.

To explain, I will again first outline the approach before illustrating with the 105 reports example.

Approach: Ask four key questions

To dig in here and understand more fully what this means, ask four questions about these stakeholders:

- ▶ What is their role?
- ▶ Who are they really?
- ▶ What else is on their mind?
- ▶ What do they think about your issue?

What is their role?

The seniority and specialty of your key audience members affects the type of content you need to include, as well as the level of detail required.

Boards skew their focus more toward strategy, with leaders having a greater focus on operations within the context of the agreed strategy. Leaders, of course, also contribute to developing that strategy in the first place.

To help clarify the distinctions between senior leaders and boards, I explain the role of each here. I begin with advisory boards, before discussing the roles of governance boards, committees and senior leaders.

Advisory boards provide help leaders think through issues

The easiest way to think about advisory boards is that they have 'all care and little responsibility'. These boards include experts who bring a specialist or strategic perspectives. They provide current knowledge, critical thinking and analysis to help leaders think through complex issues and make decisions.

At the time of writing, I am a member of the Advisory Board for Sydney's University of Technology Executive MBA Program. This board consists of a diverse mix of industry members, start-up founders and alumni. Program leaders bring issues to us and invite us to comment. These issues range from helping clarify the value proposition for the program, marketing ideas and others. We use our knowledge and relationships to help wherever we can.

Typically advisory boards will have a chair who works closely with the business leadership and facilitates the meetings. Advisory boards are at times set up for relatively short periods of time to help leaders address pressing issues, and a great deal of flexibility exists in how they operate.

Even though advisory boards typically have a well-organised structure and charter, they have zero decision-making rights or responsibilities.

Governance boards maintain a finely tuned balance between strategy and operations

Governance boards focus more on the strategic direction of the company and ensuring it meets its governance requirements. Led by a chair, this experienced group of people oversees an organisation's governance. It helps to understand three things here – firstly, a board's role; secondly, responsibilities of individual directors; and, thirdly, your own board.

Understand the board's role

The most useful explanation of the board's role I have found comes from *Standards for the Board: Improving the effectiveness of your board*, published by the UK Institute of Directors. This text explains the finely tuned balance boards must maintain between a high-level view and the operational detail.

Boards must be:

▶ entrepreneurial and yet drive the business forward while keeping it under prudent control

▶ sufficiently knowledgeable about the workings of the company to be answerable for its actions, and yet to stand back from day-to-day management and retain an objective, longer term view

▶ sensitive to the pressures of short-term local issues and yet informed of broader trends and competition, often of an international nature

▶ focused on the commercial needs of the business while acting responsibly toward employees, business partners and society as a whole.

It helps to remember that your board members may focus on your organisation for a few hours each month outside board meetings.

Having said that, a 2014 McKinsey & Company survey outlined in the article 'High-performing boards: what's on their agenda?' found higher and lower impact directors each spend about four days per year on compliance activities. Higher impact board members spend an extra eight workdays a year on strategy and about an extra three workdays on performance management, mergers and acquisitions, organisational health and risk management.

As one board director commented, his position requires him to have a 'long nose and short fingers'. In other words, he needs to have strong instincts for areas of the business that need attention while not meddling in its operations.

Become familiar with individual directors' roles

Regardless of how long or short board directors' noses and fingers are, they will be required to comply with the relevant legislation. In Australia, this is the Corporations Act and your jurisdiction will have a similar Act. At a high level (and using layman's terms) this includes the following sorts of considerations:

▶ acting for a proper purpose, which means they must vote in the interests of the company and not of themselves

- acting in good faith, which means they must genuinely believe they are acting in the company's best interests, being honest, reasonable and ethical
- acting with care and diligence, which means they must exercise their powers and discharge their duties with care and diligence; they must also display sound business judgement
- avoiding conflicts of interest, which means they must not undertake personal or professional activities that may not be in line with the interests of the company
- preventing insolvent trading, which means they must have a solid view of the company's debt position at all times
- conducting administrative duties as required.

Learn about your own board

In understanding any board I am working with, I like to find the members on LinkedIn to become familiar with their career narrative and areas of expertise. While many directors keep this deliberately slim, it is a useful place to start. I also find the latest copy of the annual report and review the director bios provided there. This will typically highlight why a particular director has been chosen for that board.

These sources, combined with speaking with the company secretary and any board members I have the chance to meet personally, help me understand the individual board members' strengths as well as their areas of interest and influence.

Understanding each director's style as well as the dynamics of the board as a group is also worthwhile. Like any team, each director has different ways of working, and different expectations and styles. Just because you have engaged successfully with one board does not mean you will have more or less success with another. They vary markedly.

A word of warning here, also: I suggest you don't rely on a single person's perspective, particularly if you are putting forward a sensitive proposal. We all have biases and you will do well to avoid being caught by those of your key stakeholders. Ask the opinions of as many people as you can to get a fully rounded view of individual directors and also board dynamics.

I have, for example, heard very different opinions from different people in a business. Some might say that a director is 'difficult' or challenging. Another may say the same person asked terrific questions that helped them think about their issue in new ways. It will depend upon your perspective and your situation as to whether this is a positive or not.

Board committees oversee specific areas

Not all boards have committees, but many do so it is worth understanding what they are for. If you are preparing an audit report, for example, you will most likely send it to the audit committee before it goes to the board. The audit committee will dive more deeply into it than the governance board will do, and the governance board will be informed by the audit committee's view of the paper and issue.

Please note that I do not suggest here that general board members will completely defer to the committee's perspective. All board members have an obligation to be across the issues of the day and to offer their opinions where necessary.

Board committees examine and debate issues related to specific areas of expertise. By going deeply into these areas, these committees enable the board as a whole to keep their eyes on the bigger picture. These committees typically consist of directors with a special interest or expertise in a particular issue. They may also invite senior executives to participate – for example, the head of audit may join the audit committee.

Many of these committees are always in place, while others can 'pop up' for short periods of time. The sorts of issues that longer term committees focus on include:

▶ audit, finance and/or budget
▶ marketing and public relations
▶ product or program development
▶ remuneration and/or people development.

Short-term committees can focus on a wide range of topics. Here are some examples:

▶ major events
▶ research
▶ CEO transition or search
▶ site relocation
▶ capital campaign or perhaps initial public offering.

This is not a complete list, but it gives you some ideas. Your organisation's annual report will include a list of its committees and members. Individual directors may also call these out in their LinkedIn profiles.

Senior leadership teams bring a wide range of perspectives to address strategy and operations for the whole organisation

Your CEO will likely have a seat on the board and act as the primary conduit between the board and the leadership team. They will work closely with the board chair in deciding what sorts of information the board needs, feeding this information to the leadership team.

Senior leadership teams include leaders from different areas of your organisation. They will include a mix of specialties, with some members being deep experts in their area and others having a generalist, potentially strategy, background.

Understanding the role each of these areas plays within your broader organisational strategy combined with the individual preferences of these leaders is key.

In understanding the needs of your senior leadership team, it helps to know as much about their performance indicators (KPIs) as possible. I like to familiarise myself with both their personal KPIs and those for their division, as well as understanding where their area fits within the whole organisation.

Your job is to help them and your broader team meet those objectives. From a theoretical perspective this is straightforward. However, practically you must know as much as possible about each person as well as their position. To complicate this, people and their positions on issues change over time – and sometimes quickly.

So, let's now think more specifically about which person or people you need to focus most on, and then get to know them.

Who are they really?

The decision-maker for your specific piece of communication may not be who you think they are. Individual roles and responsibilities, of course, play a part, but sometimes it's not so clear.

I encourage you to think about the person in your stakeholder group who will have the most influence over the decision or any consequent program delivery. The delivery matters because if they disagree with the recommendation, you risk a less-functional leadership team slowing or derailing the delivery. Someone may also have informal influence over your issue, based on their long and well-respected experience with the business.

If you are at all unclear, check in with the company secretary for the board, or your CEO's assistant if communicating to the leadership team.

What else is on their mind?

I was fascinated when speaking with a board director from a chemical company who was part of one of my board paper writing programs. When I asked what was on her mind, she said she and the other directors were very interested in a prudential inquiry into one of the major Australian banks.

She rightly thought the inquiry would lead to tighter governance requirements for all Australian boards. This in turn led to her asking for more detail about significant decisions her board needed to make to reduce the risk of falling foul of the regulator.

This means that it is important to be aware of the broader business environment, not just your specific area.

What do they think about your issue?

Each member of the leadership team or board will come to your paper with a significantly different combination of knowledge and attitudes. It's important to understand them as best you can. Here are some questions you might ask about their backgrounds and expertise before I offer a framework for thinking about their attitudes toward your message.

Understanding their backgrounds

How educated are your key decision-makers about your specific area? Are they new to the leadership team or board? Do they have domain knowledge? Are they likely to be swayed by outdated experience? Do they have a history with your project or area?

Knowing where they are coming from helps you establish how much detail you need to provide.

No member of your leadership team or board will be an expert on every issue discussed at their meeting. They will all be intelligent and curious, however, so you can be confident that in most situations they will ask decent questions.

Understanding their attitudes

Once comfortable with who is who in this zoo, you can classify stakeholder attitudes in relation to each specific message. The following options to help you understand their likely attitude toward your message:

▶ *Champions:* Ardent supporters, likely to 'win' from your proposal, and so also likely to help you get it across the line.

▶ *Objectors:* Quite the opposite to champions. They may have one of three concerns – that they are likely to 'lose' from the changes, are philosophically opposed or perhaps don't understand them.

▶ *Neutral:* Unconcerned about the proposal, may have confidence in whatever you propose or believe that your proposal is one of many equally useful solutions.

- ▶ *Advocates:* Intellectually supportive but unlikely to go out of their way to support you. They can see the advantages, but most likely they are largely unaffected by your proposal.

As you will see, thinking this through may also influence your recommendation itself. Understanding stakeholder issues and concerns helps clarify both what is needed and what is possible.

Example: Back to the 105 reports story

My client and I used a framework I offer inside the PowerPoint Planner[5] to think his stakeholder set through.

We iterated between our initial hunch around his desired outcome and tweaked it as we thought more about each of the key stakeholders.

You can see on the coming page how we sorted the stakeholders out according to their degree of interest in and influence over this specific ask.

We did this by first brainstorming their names in section #2 and taking notes about each one.

This helped us think through who would be the most important person, or people, to persuade.

It also helped us identify what we anticipated their attitudes toward the ask might be.

Sometimes when we do this, clients are not sure where their stakeholders stand, and so need to go and find out. In this case, my client had a good feel for their views so we could keep moving forward.

---

5   ClarityFirstProgram.com/ClarityHub

#1 Clarify your desired outcome

As a result of this paper, I want the executive to approve more funding either as another $1.2 million for this year or seek to carry over into FY 24.

#2 Understand your audience

Head of Projects: Has been taking resources away and providing them to other people recently. Is in a tight spot as juggling many 'important' projects with diminished resources. Fearful of being blamed for inadequate delivery of phase 1 of the project.

Head of IT and Data: Happy to continue working on the project assuming it's given the right level of priority and doesn't over stretch their team. Likes that the new strategy doesn't drip feed random reports to them but rather relies on a clear, well-scoped plan up-front.

Head of Consumer Mortgages: Relieved to have someone coming in who can sort this project out. Has offered every kind of support needed. Trusts the new project manager to deliver. Needs to engage with regulator, so is embarrassed about lack of delivery so far. Rates this project as #1 in her area.

Head of Risk and Compliance: Very keen to get this project completed ASAP given the regulator commitment.

Operations team that provides the reports: Needs the new, more efficient reports but struggling to find capacity to implement them. They are resource constrained and have been told not to change their processes as 'solutions are coming'. Currently under cost-out pressure while facing increased workload due to the extra work required to prepare reports using the older manual process.

#3 Map your stakeholders

Degree of influence over the decision

Powerful influencers

Head of IT: Advocate – likes that it is well scoped

Head of Projects: Advocate – assuming they are given resources and can avoid taking the blame for lack of delivery so far

Others

Decision-makers

Head of Consumer Mortgages: Champion – embarrassed that the project has run over so far

Head of Risk: Champion – needs to keep regulator on side

Less powerful influencers

Operations team: Champions for bigger budgets

Project team: Neutral

Degree of interest in the issue

▶ Iterate to refine your communication strategy

Now you have drafted your desired outcome in a general sense and learned more about your key stakeholders, it's time to iterate to make sure you have really nailed it.

This small sentence has a huge impact on the message you convey and the resulting value you deliver, even though it is not written into the communication itself. If it is off base, then your message will be too.

I recently saw this play out with a senior finance executive in a bank. He was adamant that the team only needed to know what to do, not why to do it. His audience didn't agree and so refused to implement his plan.

The lesson here is instructive. He had spent so much time explaining why something was necessary to other groups, that he lost sight of where this particular group was up to in the change process.

So, if as you work through the pattern picking process you find the patterns 'feel wrong', come back to this sentence and stress test it. There is a chance the pattern will be wrong of course, but more often I find the problem lies in clarifying the desired outcome.

Here are three recommendations to help:

1. Get hyper specific about the three variables in the statement.
2. Test whether you really just need to 'inform'.
3. Maximise the value you add by making recommendations wherever you can.

Get hyper specific about each of the three variables in the statement

Continuing the same example, thinking more about the stakeholders makes it clear that the primary decision-makers were the Heads of Consumer Mortgages and Risk, rather than the whole executive group. To do that, my client and I revisited our original draft outcome:

> As a result of this **paper**, I want the **executive** to **approve another $1.2 million in funding so we can complete the project on time at the end of this financial year**.

We refined it to become more specific, calling out which of the decision-makers were most important, as follows:

As a result of this **paper**, I want the **Heads of Consumer Mortgages and Risk** to approve **another \$1.2 million in funding so we can complete the project on time at the end of this financial year**.

This is as far as we went at this stage, but as we thought further, we further refined the 'ask' to include two potential options for delivering. The final version was as follows, which better reflects the roles and responsibilities of all concerned:

As a result of this **paper**, I want the **Heads of Consumer Mortgages and Risk** to **decide whether to spend more to deliver this project in full over the coming two years or to renegotiate requirements with the regulator**.

Iterating around the desired outcome is central to confirming the stakeholder management strategy.

If, for example, you realised during this process that the decision-maker – let's choose the Head of Consumer Mortgages in this instance – was adamant that no more budget was available, you need to think hard about how to proceed.

Would you set up a one-on-one with them to brief them on the delivery challenges to stress test that point of view?

Would you go to the Head of Risk and stress test the possibility of extending the regulator's deadline?

If so, what would your purpose be for each of these conversations?

The outcome of either one of these conversations would bring you back to think again about what you need to achieve at your executive committee meeting.

So, you need to iterate back and forth between the different stages in the process as your thinking matures.

Now that you have clarity around your strategy, you can start thinking about the high-level story.

Test whether you really just need to 'inform'

Although informing is sometimes the right thing to do, adopting this as a default can be more about 'hiding' than 'adding value'. The motivations for this can be simply that you don't know if your stakeholders want information or advice, so you play it safe. They can also, however, be about passing the buck up the chain to avoid taking responsibility.

So, let's look at the key outcomes you might seek from your communication so you can double check you do *really* only need to inform.

Ask yourself why you want to inform your audience, and you will typically find the real reason you are communicating. In my experience, nine times out of ten 'informing' is only the first step toward the real outcome you seek. When informing, you are typically asking your stakeholder to do one of the following:

▶ *Action:* Undertake one or more tasks, where your audience needs little explanation as to why this action matters.

▶ *Implement:* Put something into effect where you explain what to do but the audience decides how to do it.

▶ *Know:* Be aware of something so your stakeholder can factor this knowledge into their thinking and action.

▶ *Note or Understand:* Fully appreciate something so your stakeholder can then use that understanding to decide or act.

▶ *Support:* Help someone, potentially you, to undertake an activity without undertaking the activity themselves.

Maximise the value you add by making recommendations wherever you can

You will see in a moment that I offer many more patterns for making recommendations than for informing. Given the bias I have just shared, this is unlikely to be a surprise.

To make the most of these patterns, I offer a quick codex to stress-test my definitions against your own team's expectations in case they vary in your organisation. For example, what is the difference between approving and endorsing?

When persuading, you are typically asking your stakeholder to do one of these seven things:

▶ *Agree:* To agree, regardless of their level of accountability or authority.

▶ *Approve:* To enable something they have accountability for to proceed.

▶ *Change:* To change the way something they have authority over is done.

▶ *Decide:* To choose a way forward for something they have authority over.

▶ *Endorse:* To publicly approve something that the stakeholder doesn't have accountability to deliver, but which relies upon their support.

▶ *Have or maintain confidence:* To believe you can deliver, largely based on positive past experience.

▶ *Trust:* To continue to support you, even where there may not be past examples of success.

Your organisation may have slightly different definitions. If so, adjust accordingly. Once you are comfortable that you have 'nailed' the outcome this document needs to achieve, it's time to think about what kind of story to use to tell it.

CHAPTER 4

Frame your message using patterns as a quick-start

This is where we use patterns to quickly mock up a story structure that we can then test with others.

Patterns are a wonderful way to think through your messaging without necessarily being expert in the underlying structured thinking principles.

I bring these patterns to life by introducing my Pattern Picker and stepping you through how to use it.

I'll do that in four steps by explaining how to:

▶ Narrow down which patterns to try.

▶ See how pattern picking helped us find the message for the 105 reports story.

▶ Explore how patterns have helped structure many real-world papers and presentations.

As you read through these stories, you will see that some lead to happy outcomes and others less so. In all situations, we strive for a fast and informed response that drives quality decision-making, even if the outcome isn't what you hope for.

These case studies are derived from real situations. I have merged and adapted them to maintain discretion while also being realistic.

The resulting scenarios are fictitious but hopefully relatable.

Let's now see how this plays out in the coming 12 case studies.

Pattern Picker framework

1 – CLARIFY OUTCOME	2 – REVIEW POTENTIAL MESSAGES	3 – FIND MESSAGE		4 – FRAME MESSAGE
I need my audience to ...	**To achieve that I must explain ...**	**... then pick a pattern**		**... and structure it**
> Action > Endorse > Implement > Support	Action plans How to proceed	Nike	**Do X to fix Y**	2–5 steps ordered by sequence or scale
> Know > Understand	Findings What analysis revealed	Nugget	**We found X**	2–5 points of evidence ordered by scale of importance
> Have confidence > Trust	Updates The status is green, project is going well	All is Well	**We are in good shape**	2–5 reasons why we are in good shape, ordered by task or time
> Agree > Approve > Change > Decide > Endorse	Strategies How to capture an opportunity	Golden	**Do X to capture opportunity A**	Opportunity A is attractive, X will capture it, so do X
	How to solve a problem or capture an opportunity	Make the Case	**Doing X will fix Y**	2–5 reasons explaining why X is the right way to fix Y
	How to solve a problem	Oh Dear	**Do X to solve problem Y**	Problem Y matters, but X will fix it, so do X
	Options Which options to evaluate	Short List	**Consider these for solving Y**	2–5 reasons to consider these options
	Best way to capture an opportunity or solve a problem	This or That	**Option X offers best approach**	We explored these options for solving Y, but option X is best, so implement X
	Improvements How to tackle an emerging opportunity or risk	Change Tack	**Make a change to reach goal**	Have made progress, but need to make a change to reach goal, so change direction
	How to succeed when you meet only some necessary criteria	Top up	**Top up to succeed at Y**	Succeeding at Y requires X, but we have only some of X in place, so top up

▶ Narrow down which patterns to try

Experience tells me that the verb from the desired outcome is key to narrowing down which patterns to experiment with.

To help with that, I have mapped out this connection in the framework (see left). I have also accommodated some more nuanced options in the Pattern Picker (available in the Clarity Hub[6]).

Once I have clarified my desired outcome, I go to the left column on the Pattern Picker. Here I find the verb or its synonym from my outcome statement and move to the column to the right. In some cases, this takes me directly to a pattern; in others, it provides options.

If, for example, my verb is 'know' or 'understand', my path is easy. I am sharing findings from my analysis, which I can use the Nugget pattern for.

If my verb is 'decide' or 'agree', I have more patterns to choose from. To make my choice, I first ask myself what kind of things I must explain. Do I need to discuss a new strategy, options or improvements? What will be the primary focus for this communication?

This then leads me to one or more patterns to try. If I need to capture a strategic opportunity, I can choose between Make the Case and Golden. In that case, my decision making path looks like this:

1. Clarify outcome –> decide.
2. Review potential patterns –> strategies –> Golden or Make the Case.
3. Pick one and sketch out the story using this as a guide; possibly try both at a high level to see which 'feels better'.
4. Check the messaging is robust and that the tone is right for the audience. With strategies in particular, you may think that all three options might convey your message. The differentiator becomes tone. Golden, for example, is upbeat while Oh Dear is attention grabbing and strong, potentially negative too. Make the Case could be either, depending upon how you frame the supporting points.

I'll now now illustrate how this works using the 105 reports story as an example.

---

6   ClarityFirstProgram.com/ClarityHub

▶ See how patterns helped find the message for the 105 reports story

In the last chapter, I introduced our primary case study, where a program manager needed to fix a derailed project. He needed to transition 105 compliance reports from a legacy system to a new system.

So far we have thought through the desired outcome for the 105 reports story, refining our thinking about our objective and which stakeholders are central to achieving it.

Once this was clear enough, we started thinking about the structure of the paper. We could have worked bottom-up by laying out the facts and grouping and sorting our ideas to arrive at the structure.

But, we decided to try a pattern first, and marry that with our bottom-up understanding of the facts later.

I'll describe our approach first, before working step by step through the example.

Approach: We picked patterns to sketch out the high-level structure first

We took a quick look at the Pattern Picker to see what might work without being picky.

We then 'coloured the patterns in' with the information at hand, iterating to either improve that version or test a new one if our high-level skeleton didn't seem quite right.

In this example, we iterated around the high-level structure four times. This is a fairly common amount of hacking for a paper of this nature. We also used the hacking process to further refine our communication strategy.

In this situation, the refinements were important but not so great that we felt our overall path was wrong.

In some situations where our thinking is mature this 'hacking' process will involve just two rounds. In others we might do up to 10 rounds.

Lots of rounds signals that significantly more thinking is needed around both the strategy and the content to land your messaging.

Once the pattern clicks into place, I then move on to the next slide in the PowerPoint planner and flesh out the full message map.

I'll now bring this to life by illustrating how we 'hacked' the 105 reports story.

Example: We landed the messaging in four steps, while further improving the desired outcome

Here is how we did it. Let's bring back our earlier understanding of the desired outcome:

> As a result of this paper, I want the Heads of Consumer Mortgages and Risk to **APPROVE** another $1.2 million in funding so we can complete the 105 reports on time at the end of this financial year.

We scanned the left-hand column of the Pattern Picker to find patterns for stories that require approval.

Given my client felt the team needed to lean into the problem and 'fix the reports' within the regulator's time frame, Top Up seemed like a good place to start.

Here's how we thought it through to help the notes on the coming page make sense:

Step 1. Top Up quickly felt wrong. The first point, the statement, was not substantive enough and was known to the audience. It didn't belong below the main message. The top-line supporting points and those below them should only introduce ideas that are news.

Step 2. We quickly moved onto Oh Dear and kept iterating around that until we got

pretty close in version three. You can see how our thinking firms up if you review the three 'hacks'.

- Our first 'go' was helpful for the wrong reasons. It enabled my client to vent his frustrations. When seeing the thoughts on paper, it became clear that it was indelicate, and unlikely to be persuasive.
- The second attempt was better, but still not right. The first main point, the statement was thin on substance and felt belligerent.
- The third reframed the problem so it was both constructive and strong. It also led to an important shift in the desired outcome, more accurately reflecting roles and responsibilities of everyone involved. Here's what it became:

> As a result of this paper, I want the Heads of Consumer Mortgages and Risk to **DECIDE** whether to spend more to deliver the 105 reports in full over the coming two years or to renegotiate requirements with the regulator.

Now the ideas had clicked it was time to add detail, so we moved to the one-page message map.

Step 3. We then further tweaked Oh Dear once we transitioned into the message map, tightening the messaging and elevating our synthesis. You can see quite

We hacked four potential patterns before choosing Oh Dear Version 3

1 – Top up – The first point, the statement was known, so we moved it to the introduction (as you can see in the message map on the coming page)

- [STATEMENT] Meeting regulatory requirements requires us to transition all 105 legacy reports into the case system
- [COMMENT] However, we need extra funding to deliver the 105 reports (fixed scope)
- [RECOMMENDATION] Therefore, we must review funding:
  - Funding flex
  - Schedule
  - Resources

2 – Oh Dear v1 – The statement was indelicate

- [STATEMENT] The reason the reports were not delivered over the past two years was that the scoping was inadequate
- [COMMENT] However, now we have accurate scoping, we can consider several tradeoffs that will enable us to deliver reports
- Therefore, consider tradeoffs

3 – Oh Dear v2 – Getting closer but the statement too thin and felt belligerent

- [STATEMENT] We can't deliver the 105 reports within the current funding window (explain why not)
- [COMMENT] However, we can deliver some of the reports by making tradeoffs along two dimensions to proceed with the project:
  - Deliver everything in FY23 – Funding flex
  - Deliver some in FY23, some in FY24 – Schedule, scope FY23 flex and funding flex for FY24
- [RECOMMENDATION] Therefore, decide which tradeoffs to make

4 – Oh Dear v3 – Better tone, room to describe options in middle section

- [STATEMENT]: Despite testing all budgets, the 105 regulatory reports can't be delivered within the $2m budget during FY23 (explain why not – we have stress-tested the budgets)
- [COMMENT] However, we can deliver some of the reports by reprioritising funding in FY23 and FY24:
  - Deliver everything in FY23 with $1.2m more during FY23
  - Deliver some in FY23, some in FY24 with $2m or more in total
  - Deliver only the top 70 reports by FY23 (fix 36, do another 35ish)
- [RECOMMENDATION] Therefore, decide which tradeoffs to make:
  - Increase funding?
  - Pay more for the total project?
  - Accept the top 70 reports in FY23 is adequate?
  - Seek extensions from the regulator?

Annotated 105 reports message map

Meeting regulatory requirements requires us to transition all 105 legacy reports into the case system by the end of this financial year. We have now reviewed the work plans and received updated estimates.

The 'what' above emerged as from our initial pattern hacking. It comes from our first attempt with the Top Up pattern.

We are now ready to share those estimates with you along with potential ways forward.

What are you suggesting?

Delivering the 105 reports means either investing $1.2 million to $2 million more over the coming two years or renegotiating requirements with the regulator.

This main message emerged after the rest of the story came together. It offers a point of view, even though its not a decision in itself.

Despite stress testing all budgets, we can't transition all 105 regulatory reports within the agreed $2 million budget this financial year.	This means we need to make trade-offs when finalising the project workplans.	Therefore, we ask you to advise which tradeoffs we can make.
Updated estimates for database came back at **$2m,** which is 2.5 x the original budget due to a more comprehensive holistic scoping. **Budgets for other aspects of the work have not materially changed.** • Workflow remains same. • API linking ditto. • Operational teams ditto. **Work required for reports identified since June last year has not been factored in.**	We could spend $1.2m to $2m more over the coming two years. • We could deliver everything in FY23 with $1.2m more during FY23, or • We could deliver some in FY23, some in FY24 with $2m or more in total. **We could renegotiate scope or time with the regulator.** • We could deliver only the top 70 reports by FY23 (fix existing 36, do another 35ish) within the current budget, or • We could seek agreement from the regulator to further extend the project and deliver all at a later date.	Decide whether to spend more ... • Decide whether to increase funding by $1.2m for FY23. • Decide whether to budget $2m more for the project in total and roll into next year. **Decide whether to renegotiate ...** • Decide whether to pitch the regulator to accept the top 70 reports as as adequate in FY23. • Decide whether to seek extensions from the regulator. These supporting points use repetitive language to test that the ideas are parallel. We edit this out when transitioning into document format.

a lift in the messaging quality from the hacked version to the final version.

Step 4. We used some of the ideas from our initial 'go' at Top Up to introduce the story. We did this because it seemed like a sensible place to start in that it introduced relevant information about the reports project that was known by the audience. Because it was known, it did not need detailed explanation.

As you saw on page 56, we deliberately avoided typing over each draft as we iterated, but kept them next to each other to allow for healthy discussion and debate.

I have laid this out on the coming page just as we did real-time, adding colour coding to help you link our notes to the message map on the following page.

Once you have reviewed these, it's time to see how these ideas applied to the case studies I promised.

▶ Explore how patterns have helped structure many real-world papers and presentations

You might think patterns are too abstract and general to be useful. In this section, I demonstrate how practical they can be by sharing at least one real-world use case for each pattern.

This collection of stories comes from diverse organisational settings, yet together offers a proxy for a list of issues a senior team might discuss in a meeting.

In each case, I explain how the case studies came together, by:

▶ clarifying the communication strategy to be confident in what our paper or presentation will achieve

▶ synthesing the information to deliver a clear and insightful message

▶ visualising the message within the end product so decision-makers could find the message and the logic.

I first outline the two patterns that inform audiences about either what to do or what was found – Nike and Nugget – and then move on to the more extensive list of patterns that persuade.

Here's a preview with page numbers to help you find relevant examples now, and also later when you want a reference to help think through a communication.

Patterns that inform by explaining what to do or what was found:

–   Nike for explaining how to proceed *(page 59)*
–   Nugget for explaining what you found *(page 62)*

Patterns that persuade regarding progress or recommendations:

–   **Updates -** *All is Well for two things:*
    •   explaining that you are in good shape for a project *(page 65)* and
    •   offering a routine status update *(page 68)*
–   **Strategies**
    •   Golden for recommending how to capture an opportunity *(page 71)*
    •   Oh Dear for recommending how to solve a new problem *(page 73)*
    •   Make the Case for recommending how to capture an opportunity or solve a problem *(page 76)*
–   **Options**
    •   Short List for recommending which options to explore *(page 80)*
    •   This or That for recommending which option is best *(page 83)*
–   **Improvements**
    •   Change Tack for recommending how to tackle an emerging opportunity or risk *(page 88)*
    •   Top Up for recommending a new way to meet your goal *(page 91)*

Patterns that inform by explaining what to do or what was found

The Nike and Nugget patterns help when you need your audience to do or know something, and when little persuasion is needed. Let's now bring these to life.

Nike drives for action

| Do X to fix Y | 2 to 5 steps ordered by scale or sequence |

Nike offers an opportunity to put forward a new action plan for an audience that does not need significant persuasion.

Nike thrives where a proposition is simple and easily understood. It allows you to say, 'Here's what we think we should do', and then support each point with a list of actions explaining how each one will deliver on a specific objective.

When deciding whether this pattern is right, refer back to your outcome statement and look for verbs such as 'implement', 'action', 'support' or similar.

The example in this section comes from the head of learning and development (L&D) at a global consulting firm. I work through each of the three message structuring phases, describing the following:

- *Strategise:* To seek approval to pilot a promising revenue-lifting program.
- *Synthesise:* Action-oriented Nike suited the simplicity of the proposal.
- *Visualise:* The message was delivered via a simple prose paper.

The strategy was to seek approval to pilot a potentially revenue-lifting program

The strategy was simple: to get approval and get going. Breaking that down, the head of L&D and I drafted the following statement:

> 'As a result of this presentation, I want the partnership to ENDORSE an $80K budget to run a pilot program to help new partners each deliver an extra $500K in revenue over their first year.'

The narrative did not need to explain why this was the right number or how this had come about. Finding a relatively low-cost way to increase the revenue generation capability of new partners had been discussed at the previous partnership meeting.

L&D had taken the initiative to design a solution for that problem and was ready to share their recommendation at the next meeting.

Action-oriented Nike suited the simplicity of the proposal

The communication outlined a simple ask explaining how the team would achieve the desired result in a low-risk way.

In my experience, partnership groups are eager to invest in small ways to lift their revenue. The downside risk of this proposal was so small, risks were not considered worthy of discussion.

You can see how it came together on page 61, to the right.

The message was delivered as a simple prose paper

Once the ideas were clear, the author converted the messaging into a simple prose paper to be used as pre-reading for the coming partnership meeting. Given the partnership preferred prose communication, this was a natural choice.

My client received immediate approval for her recommendation and has since run a successful pilot program, which has been rolled out more widely across the firm.

Nike explaining how to lift profitability

This year we agreed to change the shape of our client base and focus on dynamic and profitable clients. Global leadership has identified 12 key practice areas and continues to scan for practice areas with global growth potential.

We have a proposal that will help us seize growth opportunities in key areas.

How can we seize these potential global growth opportunities?

Invest $80K in a pilot to accelerate the profitability of 15 promising new partners so they deliver a combined $7.5m more in their first year.

Invest $80K in a program to increase profitability of new partners by $500K each per year from year one.	Work closely with participants to refine pilot program and assess effectiveness.	Scale up and design for ongoing program delivery to other key practice areas.

Invite leadership to identify 15 promising new partners from one of the 12 priority practice areas and nominate at least one sponsor.
 	
Endorse Learning and Development (L&D) investing $80K in program to help new partners develop a personal business development (BD) action plan.
 	
• Global partners to offer sector and BD guidance, highlighting easy sales opportunities that new partners often miss.
• BD coach participants on nuances of their sector to acclerate their sales skills.
• L&D to teach how to use BD tools when focusing on new business targets.
• L&D to gain participants' commitment to deliver on their individual $500K goal, aligning them with a typical mid-earning 2nd year partner.
	• BD to monitor participants' engagement every two months to offer support and check progress against their plan.
	• L&D to drive progress over the coming year by
	  ▪ keeping participants accountable to individual action plans quarterly and measuring success by profitability and/or new engagements opened
	  ▪ measuring the revenue achievements of the 15 participants over their first year in the program
	  ▪ offering regular online cohort catchups to cement group cohesion, share successes and related strategies while firming their commitment to BD.
	• L&D to report to leadership quarterly and adjust program settings accordingly.
		• Identify next three practice areas to roll the program out for over the following year.
		• Create a plan for ongoing program delivery.
		• Launch marketing and communications to encourage ideas from partners on emerging areas.
		• Share program successes widely to encourage active participation from future cohorts and support from senior partners to release new partners to participate.

Nugget creates knowledge and understanding

We found X	2 to 5 points of evidence ordered by scale

The Nugget pattern enables analysts to outline their findings without offering a recommendation. Even though the main message is not an action or a recommendation, it still qualifies as an insight. It goes beyond laying out the facts to offer a point of view about those facts.

A clue that leads me to choose Nugget is seeing verbs such as 'know' or 'understand' in the outcome statement.

This example comes from the energy sector. The senior leadership team asked the analytics team to review the risks associated with different forms of renewable energy. Given they were asked to conduct research and deliver findings rather than a recommendation, Nugget was the perfect choice. I unpack the example in three parts:

- ▶ *Strategise:* The strategy was limited to explaining the key findings to the leadership team.
- ▶ *Synthesise:* The Nugget story explained why wind energy posed more risks than other options.
- ▶ *Visualise:* The message was delivered as a presentation.

The strategy was limited to explaining the key findings to the leadership team

Less effort is required to think through a strategy that only needs to deliver research insights.

The goal is to articulate the findings clearly and insightfully to allow your audience to decide what to do with them. This involves understanding how much your audience knows about the topic already to help calibrate the amount of detail you need. If you know that some among your audience have light understanding or strong views about the subject, you may want to provide extra detail or alert your senior stakeholders so they can manage that.

The desired outcome for this example reads as follows:

> 'As a result of this paper, I want the senior leadership team to UNDERSTAND that wind energy poses great risks to our portfolio.'

Nugget explained why wind energy posed more risk than other options

I chose this example because it is so simple and relatable. Even without getting into the numbers sitting underneath each of the points, you can easily follow the argument and I hope apply the approach to your own research.

I like the way the supporting points are organised here, initially explaining why wind is relevant to the portfolio, explaining the problem with wind and then going further to explain why the problems with wind matter.

I add one caveat. You would ordinarily expect the senior leadership team (SLT) to know what proportion of their renewable energy came from each source. In this case, the SLT included three new non-technical leaders who came from outside the sector. The researchers decided to first explain the importance of wind to the portfolio to help these new leaders catch up while also updating the other SLT members on the specific details.

I generally caution against 'backgrounding everyone'. In this case it was fitting because the rest of the team were keen to update their understanding of their renewables status. More commonly I suggest updating the new SLT or board members separately to protect the rest of the group from duplication.

Please note that in the message map on page 64, I generalised the numbers to reflect the whole Australian energy market to protect confidentiality.

This message was delivered as a presentation

The presentation first offered an executive summary calling out the top line messaging before offering several charts for each section of the story. It included an overview of the research methodology in the appendix for those who were interested in that level of detail.

The team provided the whole deck including this appendix as pre-reading before attending the meeting to answer questions, which turned out to be minimal.

The discussion quickly moved toward a request for a separate paper from the Energy Trading Team concerning opportunities for protecting against energy volatility generated by wind droughts.

Patterns that persuade

You need to persuade senior leaders for broadly two reasons: to gain trust during updates or gain their support for a recommendation. In this section, I begin with case studies for gaining trust before moving onto recommendations.

Delivering some nuggets of insight

Our part of the Future Proofing Project is to identify risks and opportunities of a future energy market, which we expect to be dominated by renewables.

We have now completed the Phase 2 analysis and are ready to provide our results.

What did you find?

Wind droughts present a great and persistent risk to energy reliability and our portfolio.

Wind forms a large component of our renewable energy portfolio.	Wind droughts can be significant and widespread at key times of the year.	Wind unreliability can't yet be mitigated against.
<ul><li>Wind in 2023 provided 10% of our total energy and 37.5% of the renewable energy supply, having increased its contribution by an average of 15% per year for the past decade.</li><li>Solar provided 12% of our total energy supply.<ul><li>Small scale solar has been growing at approximately 29% per year over the past 10 years.</li><li>Large scale solar has rapidly expanded since 2016 and now offers 4% of total generation.</li></ul></li><li>Hydro contributed a steady 6%.</li><li>Geothermal is not yet in production, although promising experiments are being conducted in the Northern Territory.</li></ul>	Wind droughts can last for up to 14 days at a time, placing significant stress on the system.<ul><li>There were many incidents where outages lasted for seven days.</li><li>There was one incident where an outage lasted for 14 days.</li></ul>Wind droughts can occur across wide distances, particularly during late Q1 and into Q2. We found one incident where all three stations across the southern seaboard showed no wind for seven days.	<ul><li>Battery storage won't work given the difficulty of sourcing and locating sufficient batteries to offset the magnitude of lulls in energy driven by such significant wind droughts.</li><li>Interconnection won't work as wind droughts occur simultaneously across wide areas of the country, removing the possibility of drawing energy from other locations.</li><li>Coal and gas do not classify as renewable energy sources, and so are out of scope.</li><li>Nuclear is not available in Australia, and unlikely to be approved by the current government and so is a long shot.</li></ul>

Updating regarding a project's progress or an area's current status

All is Well is great for updating stakeholders on progress when projects are performing well. I offer two examples here to highlight the variety of uses. The first is a project update and the second is a routine 'business as usual' or BAU status update. The BAU example showcases how to use All is Well for an 'amber' rather than 'bright green' story, to bring in a bit of extra real-world complexity.

Either way, the goal is to create trust. You might wonder why I have created a pattern that is all about trust.

Why not just 'provide an update'?

'Updating' on its own is all about you, the presenter, when instead you want to focus on the audience. So, when I ask *why* you need to update someone about a project that is progressing well, people tell me that they want the continued confidence of their leadership. In other words, they want the leadership to trust them to deliver.

Often when I scratch more deeply by asking 'Why do you want to update them?', we find hidden requests for support or funding.

This naturally leads to a different pattern choice.

However, if the project is performing well, you will primarily want to create confidence or trust. I'll now showcase the classic All is Well structure for a project update before sharing a BAU status update.

All is Well to create confidence that a project is progressing well

We are in good shape	2 to 5 reasons ordered by task or time

All is Well is a simple structure for updating stakeholders on the progress of a program of work when it is in good shape. It is a 'nothing to see here' story that seeks a change in direction.

In this example the Chief Marketing Officer needs to update the SLT on the status of a culture improvement project. BigTech leadership has realised their existing culture is fragmented and does not align with their current strategic ambitions. What worked years ago for an engineering-led consultancy does not serve the customer-oriented technology solution provider it has become.

The SLT and board agreed to hire BrandCo to work with them on this. I explain in three parts:

1. *Strategise:* To maintain trust among the SLT and board, particularly the lukewarm CTO.

2. *Synthesise:* All is Well demonstrated that the project was in good shape.
3. *Visualise:* The message was delivered as a paper for noting.

I'll now discuss each of these, one by one.

The strategy was to maintain trust among the SLT and board, particularly the lukewarm CTO

While the SLT and board unanimously support the need to renew the BigTech's corporate identity, the CTO and CFO are not convinced that BrandCo can deliver. They respect the consultancy's reputation in general terms, but found their pitch to be 'a bit fluffy' and light on concrete success metrics.

So, the CMO is alert to the need for transparency to maintain full support for the project's process and outcomes.

As a result, the CMO's desired outcome went like this:

> 'As a result of this noting paper, we want the whole SLT but particularly the CTO and CFO to MAINTAIN CONFIDENCE that the corporate identity process is on track to deliver material benefit to the organisation.'

All is Well demonstrated that the project was in good shape

Given this is a noting paper sharing the good news that the project is on track, All is Well is the perfect choice. This pattern allowed the author to explain to the SLT what has been done, what they were currently doing and what they have planned for the coming period.

The author focused the middle section on the four draft success criteria to highlight their commitment to specific – and not fluffy – results. This was appropriate because confirming these criteria was the current focus of the work, and convenient because it helped counter the CTO's concerns.

If you read the messaging on page 67 closely, you will see that the ideas are organised by time, with the completed items being outlined first, then the current issues followed by the future plans.

The message was delivered as a paper for noting

The authors delivered this as a two-page prose paper for noting. As they had hoped, discussion wasn't needed at the SLT meeting because all members were satisfied with the project's progress.

Creating confidence that 'All is Well' with this project's progress

BigTech's corporate identity has evolved from our early days as a small engineering-led consultancy and has not kept pace with our evolution into a large, customer-oriented software business.

It is time to update you on our progress at this early stage of our 12-week corporate identity project.

How is the project progressing?

The BrandCo project is making good progress toward better aligning our corporate identity with our strategy.

In December we began work with BrandCo to help us better understand and articulate our corporate identity.	We have developed four draft criteria in our continuing effort to clarify what a successful corporate identity entails for us.	We will continue to work with BrandCo over January and February to renew our corporate identity.
We allocated a budget of $X to support a team of five to run the project.	1. The renewed corporate identity aligns with BigTech's strategic ambitions.	January will involve the initial desktop review, Kickoff workshops and senior leadership discussions.
We met on 10 December with the senior BrandCo team to lay foundations for the project.	2. The renewed corporate identity resonates with the SLT and board.	February will focus on interviews and workshops with key stakeholder groups before reconvening with the SLT late in the month.
• We clarified key questions they were to explore and landed on the following three: ▪ What role does corporate identity play for BigTech? ▪ How does each stakeholder group currently articulate our corporate identity? ▪ How can we leverage these perspectives to articulate a new identity that resonates widely? • We determined the scope of the project would include helping us bring the new identity to life for employees, suppliers and customers once it was clarified.	3. The renewed corporate identity statement is sufficiently aspirational to motivate staff, catchy enough to attract customers and practical enough to guide decisions at all levels of the organisation. 4. The renewed corporate identity is feasible for BigTech to implement within six months and with less than $3m in cash spend to execute.	February will involve iterating the MVP (minimum viable product) language and design with focus groups before finalising the corporate identity and rollout plan.

All is well for maintaining confidence during a routine safety update

We are in good shape	2 to 5 reasons ordered by task or time

I include this extra example because governing large organisations requires a large volume of these kinds of routine papers across many different areas.

The volume of complaints about these papers coming from senior leaders and boards is also high!

Senior leaders and boards often complain that they receive screeds of data about the status of different parts of the organisation that they themselves are then required to analyse and summarise before they can make sense of the organisation's real position.

This difficulty can be exaccerbated by the reporting templates that prevail for these kinds of updates. I will talk more about handling these later, but for now think about this example as the executive summary.

This safety update from a large retailer outlines how All is Well can help deliver not only clearer but also more insightful routine status reports.

Here's how I will walk through this example:

- ▶ *Strategise:* To provide comfort that the safety results were accurate and improving.
- ▶ *Synthesise:* All is Well highlighted the steadily improving safety performance.
- ▶ *Visualise:* The executive summary was delivered before area by area results.

The strategy was to provide comfort that the safety results were accurate and improving

The key was to garner trust in the accuracy of the results, rather than to persuade the decision-makers to act.

Whether you need to 'update' or 'recommend' becomes a finely tuned judgement call for executives from risk and governance functions. In this example, the Chief Safety Officer decided 'updating' was the right path to take. He did not need to recommend a change of plan but rather support more of the same.

As a result, his desired outcome read like this:

'As a result of the Q2 safety update, I want the senior leadership team to HAVE CONFIDENCE that the organisation's safety performance is improving.'

You can see how the story came together on page 69.

Giving confidence that 'All is Well' through a BAU safety report

Last quarter we explained that our safety performance was static, despite significant risks associated with unusually high staff turnover and a 10% lift in sales volume across many stores stemming from the holiday season.

We have now reviewed our safety and health performance for Q2.

What is our safety and health performance like for Q2?

Our safety performance improved significantly during Q2, although opportunities exist to further reduce risk.

The number of serious incidents remained steady and small, although the severity level has reduced.	The number of employee injuries has reduced significantly, although we have mixed results in relation to meeting this year's target.	Our half yearly valuation of the provisions needed for settling common law claims is in line with the expected $5m increase.	Our annual audit review highlights the need to more closely align our audit framework with that of our external auditor to reduce risk.
We have experienced one armed hold-up this quarter, versus four last quarter. • Larger and more visible security presence at the entry of at-risk stores appears to be deterring potential offenders from undertaking hold-ups. • Incentives to encourage customers to pay with cards have reduced the cash in store, potentially making our stores a less attractive hold-up target. We have experienced five personal injury incidents involving falling fixtures and fittings across supermarkets and liquor stores, compared with two last quarter. (list incidents)	• 18.8% fewer employees were injured at work and needed to take more than one shift off this year, but we missed target by 4.3%. • 12.5% fewer employees were injured at work and needed to take one shift off than last year, which is in line with target. • 16.2% fewer employees suffered workplace injuries that did not require time off than last year and was 3.76% better than target.	• We have experienced an increase in the Workers Compensation claims and settlement sizes in Washington, which increases the exposure by approximately $10 million. Other states are flat. • We have experienced a drop in Public Liability claims over the quarter, dropping exposure by $5 million year to date.	• Internal audits focus primarily on preventing the most significant risks that impact our license to operate. • However, the external auditor focuses on the total number of risks that expose our suppliers, customers and employees to risk. • Therefore, we need to more closely align our internal audit framework to with external auditors' expectations. NOTE: The dot points in this section are organised differently. This isn't just a 'list' of points. It's a logical argument. I'll explain how this different 'deductive' structure works shortly.

All is Well highlighted the steadily improving safety performance

This story walked a fine line between familiarity and flexibility. It retained a familiar cadence to help the audience compare against similar past reports while not stifling the message.

This CSO walked that line with aplomb, offering the two metrics reported on every quarter first, before then moving on to a half yearly and an annual topic.

The executive summary was delivered before area by area results

As with many routine updates, the deck was substantial. At 60 slides long it provided a depth of information around all of the safety metrics the organisation reported against.

The executive summary called out the highlights that the CSO believed mattered most to the decision-makers at that point. He ran through these at the start of the meeting and then dipped in and out of the remaining 58 slides, which summarised the state of safety across the business over the past quarter, to answer questions.

As expected, the SLT accepted his update and agreed to continue their existing strategies for improving performance.

Recommending new strategies

So far, I have introduced stories that follow the same underpinning grouping structure to deliver action plans, findings and updates. This foundational structure is simple: it offers one main message that is supported by a small number of points that are independent of each other.

If I visualise this structure, it looks like this:

Grouping: For almost any type of message supported by individual ideas

I now introduce two patterns that use a different underlying structure, based on deductive logic.

Building a case using deductive logic requires three supporting points, with the first two outlining your reasoning that convinces your audience in your recommendation. Once they accept your reasoning, they will be ready for your implementation plan. Here is how I visualise that structure:

Deductive: For recommendations supported by chained reasons and an action

The coming three 'strategy patterns' use a mix of grouping and deductive structures to make recommendations.

I first cover two deductive patterns, Golden and Oh Dear, and then discuss Make the Case, which uses a grouping structure.

Golden for explaining how to capture an opportunity

Do X to capture opportunity A	Opportunity A is attractive	X will capture it	Do X

Golden is for stories that excite. This pattern is for capturing new opportunities, rather than solving problems, and so is easy to deliver.

My client was working for the digital marketing team in a retailer keen to 'lift its game' in an increasingly competitive market. The CEO was part way through implementing a significant growth strategy and the team was enjoying stretching themselves to find smart ways to lift sales.

In this setting, they found an opportunity to leverage artificial intelligence that they thought was a winner. I'll run through their message in three parts as follows:

▶ *Strategise:* To excite the CEO and COO about a quick win opportunity.

▶ *Synthesise:* Golden showcased the opportunity before explaining the implementation strategy.

▶ *Visualise:* The message was delivered in a short conversation with the CEO and COO.

I'll now unpack these individually.

The strategy was to excite the CEO and COO about a quick win opportunity

The communication strategy for this narrative doesn't need much explanation. The head of digital marketing was confident they were on a 'winner' and did not see any reason the key people would knock back their recommendation.

They had done the ground work by running a pilot that the Chief Marketing Officer had supported. The pilot was successful and now it was time for broader support.

The head of digital wanted the following outcome:

> 'As a result of this meeting, I want the CEO and COO to be so excited about the opportunity for rolling out the MightyGood technology nationwide that they immediately SAY YES.'

The good news was that they did, and then asked the CMO (who was also present) to update the rest of the senior team at their upcoming weekly meeting.

Exciting leaders about a 'golden' opportunity

The digital marketing team continually scans for opportunities to optimise the return from our promotional activities.

We have found a potential quick win to bolster store sales using existing AI technology that requires little investment.

What is it?

We recommend expanding the MightyGood AI-driven advertising pilot across the whole network next month to quickly lift incremental revenue.

Better using our existing MightyGood infrastructure could deliver incremental revenue with minimal cash or human investment.	The ongoing MightyGood pilot is showing sufficient incremental uplift from upselling to higher margin items to warrant immediate network rollout.	Therefore, we recommend implementing MightyGood across all stores next month.

• Adopting AI-driven advertising would help us keep up with fresh-food peers who are also experimenting with sophisticated AI advertising approaches.
 	
• The necessary MightyGood technology and advertising is already embedded in all stores, avoiding time-consuming set-up.
 	
• The $100k monthly subscription for the extra AI feature and any extra collateral is within budget.
 	
• We can cancel the monthly subscription for the extra features we need after three months with no penalty, given our existing relationship with MightyGood.
	• AB testing indicates significant increase in sales:
	  ▪ 2x uplift on sales of coffee and sides during AI-driven weeks
	  ▪ 80% clearance of languishing fresh items in the last hour of store opening.
	
	• The pilot has required only an extra $20 in sales per day per store to cover costs.
	
	• Incremental sales uplift of $X to $Y per store cut end-of-day food waste by 70%.
	
	• Increased returns per store offers potential to lift serving staff wages.
	
	• Anecdotal customer feedback has been positive, with several occasional customers commenting the AI-driven reminders were welcome.
		• Commit to roll out to all stores this month for a minimum of three months to test that the pilot benefits hold nationwide.
		
		• Invest $100K per month from the existing advertising budget to pay the license fees.
		
		• Set up a benefits tracker model to ensure we monitor results at a granular level across the whole network.
		
		• Allow the digital marketing team to reduce time spent on Project Banana to accommodate setting up granular MightGood reporting.
		
		• Report back to SLT monthly.

Golden showcased the opportunity before explaining the implementation strategy

In retail environments, simple ways to improve sales are typically welcomed – and quickly. This is especially so on the back of a pilot that has gone well. This narrative was no different.

You can see in the message map to the left that the head of digital marketing began by highlighting the opportunity to build excitement. This set the scene for the next section, outlining why her proposal to go nationwide was the right way to capture this opportunity, which in turn readied them to support a simple action plan.

By the time they had heard the first two parts of the story, the CEO and COO were ready to hear how to roll out MightyGood nationwide.

In laying out her story so cleanly as a one-pager, she was also making it easier for her CMO to make a verbal update to the SLT.

The message was delivered in a short conversation with the CEO and COO

The head of digital marketing had just 15 minutes with the CEO and COO at the end of a monthly marketing roundup.

They deliberately kept it informal, bringing a one-page message map with them and three charts highlighting the

returns from the pilot and describing the AB testing campaigns.

Given the lack of time, the seemingly obvious benefits of her recommendation and an organisational preference for action *now*, a one-pager was a pragmatic choice and the leaders quickly agreed they should proceed with the rollout.

Having now seen how such a positive deductive structure can work, let's flip to its opposite.

Oh Dear to explain how to solve new problems

Oh Dear is wonderful for grabbing a decision-makers' attention, but requires care. It is strong, and sometimes too strong to be effective, particularly where corporate culture does not encourage confrontation.

In a recent discussion with members of my online program, a participant commented that he likes the directness of the structure. He has learned, however, that toning down the message by choosing other structures (such as This or That or Top Up, which I'll discuss shortly) can be more effective in achieving the same ends. Wherever possible, he now saves Oh Dear until he needs to draw close attention to a new problem that was not caused by anyone on the leadership team.

As this highlights, the one story can sometimes be told multiple ways. The choice comes down to matching the message with the desired outcome and tone you think will serve you best.

The coming example is at the stronger end, where a new Chief Technology Officer is calling out the cyber security problems he found on arrival in his new role at an investment house. Here's the breakdown:

1. *Strategise:* To use radical transparency to gain trust and urgent funding.
2. *Synthesise:* Oh Dear galvanised senior leaders into fast action.
3. *Visualise:* The message was delivered as a formal presentation after significant pre-engagement.

I'll now unpack these to explain how it all played out.

The strategy was to use radical transparency to gain trust and urgent funding

The CTO was mindful of the need to walk a fine line here. He was new in the role and so, although he saw an urgent need to address the investment house's cyber security vulnerability, he didn't want to be seen to trash his predecessor.

He decided to be clear and direct, balancing out any temptation to be overly bold with one-on-one conversations with all members of the leadership team before the SLT meeting. He thought carefully about the desired outcome for each of these conversations, which varied slightly according to the level of knowledge and proximity of that person to the problems he found.

By the time he got to finalise his SLT presentation, his desired outcome was:

> 'As a result of this presentation, I want the CFO and CEO to BE CONFIDENT they have the full support of the leadership team to invest heavily in an upgraded cyber security capability.'

He narrowed his focus to these two key leaders given they would be 'on the hook' for the final decision. Support from the other SLT members would amount to nought if these two did not support the investment.

Oh Dear galvanised senior leaders into fast action

By the time he prepared the paper using the message map on page 75, he was confident he understood any lingering issues among the leadership team. He was also ready to address any questions they may have about how each of the board members would respond to this

Oh Dear, we need to spend more on cyber security

Cyber security is a growing threat to our business. A recent review highlighted that our current approach is outside the board's risk tolerance.

We have prepared a holistic cyber security strategy for your consideration.

What is the strategy?

We recommend allocating $20 million to roll out a comprehensive three-year cyber security strategy.

Our cyber security approach has been piecemeal as we react to specific and individual threats.	Protecting our organisation requires investing $20 million to deliver a comprehensive cyber strategy over the coming three years.	We recommend allocating $20 million to cyber security over the coming three years.

• We are experiencing increasing numbers of threats, including three in the past year that we know of.
 • Although none of these threats have been successful, containing them is increasingly difficult.
 • Internal audit has identified that our defenses are porous.
 • We are outside the board's risk tolerance for cyber safety.
	• Our review of best practices from experts tells us we must cover six key areas.
	 • We have identified the most robust yet pragmatic ways to address those six key areas for our specific context.
	 • When implemented, the plan will bring our organisation within the board's level of risk tolerance.
	 • We have calibrated the plan carefully to optimise the $20m investment, so it protects us thoroughly without overspending.
		• Allocate $2m in Q1 to hire a small team.
		 • Allocate $10m next year to:
		   ▪ identify and patch current critical weaknesses
		   ▪ design the architecture required for a future-proof environment
		   ▪ agree monitoring protocols to allow flexibility as the threats evolve.
		 • Allocate $10m the year after to set up the systems and tools we need to protect us across all six areas.
		 • Allocate $8m the year after to embed the systems and tools across the whole business.

significant financial request. This mattered because the board would need to sign off on anything the SLT agreed on given the dollars involved.

He was deliberate in using straightforward language without hyperbole to explain the situation and his recommended solution directly and clearly.

The message was delivered as a formal presentation after significant pre-engagement

The CTO prepared a detailed prose paper for the SLT that could easily be repurposed for the board. He delivered the paper well in advance of the meeting and checked in with each SLT member informally after he thought they'd had a reasonable chance to read it and before the meeting itself.

The meeting was light on presentation and 'long' on discussion. He quickly refreshed everyone's memory around the top-line story and then settled in to answer questions.

The discussion focused almost completely around confirming substantive issues rather than clarifying what it was all about.

He left with their confidence and the CEO's support to send the proposal to the next board meeting for their support.

Make the Case for solving problems and capturing opportunities

Do X to fix Y	2 to 5 reasons this is the right strategy

Make the Case offers flexibility within a framework by helping you make a recommendation and argue the case against your chosen criteria.

It enables you to explain why both your recommendation and your rollout plan are right.

There are many ways to structure the supporting points while holding true to the principles that underpin this pattern.

You may have developed bespoke criteria for evaluating your proposal, rely on a framework your leadership has asked you to use or perhaps a domain-specific set of problem-solving critera.

One that I saw recently explained why an audit committee should accept a proposal to pay more for an insurance policy. That discussion focused around three reasons, one for each of three categories: product, price and process.

I like this one because it was rigorous while also being punchy. The use of alliteration strengthened the delivery.

Today, I share my favourite Make the Case structure. It sets you up to justify why your idea best suits the classic business needs of strategy, returns, implementation and risks.

In this instance, this framework allowed my client to be rigorous and unemotional, which was difficult in this setting given her frustration at slow decision making.

Here's the high-level story:

1. *Strategise:* To spur action by delivering a comprehensive pitch.
2. *Synthesise:* Make the Case lived up to its name, offering a powerful pitch.
3. *Visualise:* The case was delivered as a prose paper.

I'll now expand on each of these.

The strategy was to spur action by delivering a comprehensive pitch

The stakeholder management around this example was challenging, particularly as the head of the project management office was making an expedient recommendation that she did not herself like.

She believed she had previously 'pushed' for her preferred option as far as she could without success. In light of this, she just needed a solution that enabled her to manage an increasingly large and complex project portfolio.

Here is her outcome statement:

> 'As a result of this senior leadership team meeting, I want the CFO and the CTO to AGREE to urgently implement Solution Alpha to manage projects across the five project management offices.'

She did not expect significant opposition given the earlier failed efforts to persuade the leadership to adopt her preferred solution, Beta. She was to be surprised.

Make the Case lived up to its name, offering a powerful pitch

We quickly chose Make the Case. It covered all four key metrics, while being clear that Alpha was an expedient rather than ideal choice.

In contrast, a deductive pattern would have exposed her to the risk of digging more deeply into reasoning that the leadership had previously rejected or of including irrelevant material. Here is our thinking:

▶ Oh Dear would have reminded the leadership of problems they were either aware of or had caused. Our attempts to reframe our way out of this by redefining the problem did not work. None of these was helpful: the current portfolio management approach is unworkable, the current software is inadequate for the growing portfolio, or the current reporting barely meets auditor requirements.

- ▶ Top Up required the head to explain the ideal situation and how their current portfolio management approach was inadequate. This was not necessary because the SLT knew this already.
- ▶ This or That required her to compare options. She had done this already and been overruled.
- ▶ Change Tack wasn't fit for purpose because she didn't have a genuine and substantively positive statement she could make to set up the following two points.

The story on page 79 showcases the delicate balance she took to convey why urgently proceeding with Alpha was now the right way forward, despite her misgivings.

The case was delivered as a prose paper

This company prefers prose to PowerPoint, so my client stuck with protocol. Given charts and diagrams weren't central to the audience understanding the narrative, she didn't need to challenge the leaders' preferred communication style.

She included tables to outline the high-level numbers as needed and offered more detailed costings in the appendix.

Unfortunately, despite her high hopes, my client did not get the outcome she desired. To her great frustration, all SLT members bar one agreed. The one who disagreed was central to the case and he and his team had refused to engage in the decision-making process before the meeting.

She was then asked to work closely with this leader – who publicly committed to make this a priority – to confirm that her recommendation did indeed meet his requirements. Assuming that process went well, she then had the SLT's blessing to move forward. If not, she would need to make a new recommendation.

This highlights that even if a story is well structured, it can come unstuck if the surrounding stakeholder dynamics are not well managed. Sadly, this was beyond my client's control as her seniors were not providing the support she needed.

A more positive spin is that the meeting did nudge her closer to getting the result she needed, albeit more slowly than she wanted.

Making the Case for a new project management system

Last quarter, we assessed whether Alpha or Beta would be the best fit portfolio management solution for the five project management offices (PMO). The results were close. Although Beta was a better technical fit for our project management needs, it was not the preferred option given the organisational familiarity with Alpha.

We have now considered the issue further and are ready to recommend how to proceed.

How should we proceed?

Urgently proceed with Alpha to enable the five PMOs to better manage the rapidly growing project portfolio.

Alpha can meet our project management needs, enabling us to manage our rapidly growing project portfolio.	The PMO budget can accommodate the $X up-front customisation fees and $X for maintenance and support.	Alpha has stronger internal support given its wide use for discrete project management tasks.	Proceeding quickly enables the PMO to mitigate against key delays and support concerns.
Alpha's customisability enables us to build a bespoke management system that reports consistently on individual projects as well as the whole portfolio (support by listing the top-line ways the system can be customised to report consistently).

Alpha's workflow is comprehensive although it involves extra steps for key tasks.
- It can do A, but requires 10 more clicks to achieve the same outcome vs Beta.
- It can do B, although it requires three more steps to achieve the same outcome as Beta. | Configuring key project management reporting needs into Alpha will cost $X up-front, which is not required with Beta because it is a specific program management tool (support with top-line of itemised costings).

Alpha will require up to $XX operational budget annually for maintenance and support.
- $Y to $Y1 to maintain per year.
- $Z to $Z1 to support per year. | Alpha is used widely to complete discrete project management tasks.
- It is used widely for project planning.
- It is used widely for expense tracking and reporting.

Beta on prem is being phased out across the business for project timesheets.
- Costly to support.
- Costly to maintain.

Beta Cloud is not used elsewhere in the business.

IT team members key to setting up the PMO systems are familiar with and prefer Alpha. | Starting now will bring forward the anticipated 3–4 months needed to configure Alpha.
- It will take xxx time to do report A versus one week set up time for Beta.
- It will take xxx time to do report B versus one week set up time for Beta.

Starting now enables existing users to coach new users who need to master the 'average' user interface.

Starting now will enable us to begin while the existing, high-quality support provider is in place.

Starting now counters the potential uncertainty of future support raised by the recent purchase of the support vendor by BigCo, which has hinted at reducing support from 2025. |

Discussing options

Many leaders require you to to discuss optionsduring a decision-making process.

I offer two patterns to meet these requirements: Short List, to agree on which options to evaluate, and This or That, for recommending an option to pursue.

After sharing these examples I will share a framework to help you think about what structures might work at different stages of a program.

Short List for recommending which options to evaluate

Consider these to solve Y	2 to 5 reasons to consider these options

Decision-making processes frequently involve evaluating options. The scale and complexity of the decisions will dictate the types of communication required during the decision-making process.

Where the situation is complex, you will need to bring stakeholders along your decision-making journey with you.

Short List is terrific during the early stages of these journeys. It enables you to involve decision-makers in validating or potentially deciding which options your team should pursue.

In this example, I outline an early-stage discussion regarding potential growth strategies for a technology company. Here's the breakdown:

1. *Strategise:* To engage the board in prioritising options for growing revenues close to home.
2. *Synthesise:* Short List explained the benefits of two options before highlighting the risks of pushing customer acqusition.
3. *Visualise:* The CMO provided the paper in prose format as a prelude to a rich discussion.

The strategy was to engage the board in prioritising options for growing revenues close to home

This story came at an exciting time. Their product was selling well as customers came to see the advantages of a wholly cloud-based enterprise management system.

The delicacy came in keeping some of the more aggressively growth-minded board members in check. They wanted to push aggressively to acquire more customers.

The Chief Marketing Officer was concerned that their success was fragile and their reputation and results could quickly come undone if they grew too fast too soon.

He saw the need to engage the board regularly on progress as a way of incrementally educating them about the pros and cons of different growth strategies. As you will see, he did so without listing 'pros' and 'cons'. Instead, he wrapped them into the messaging.

This first communication since the strategy day was key to that engagement process. Here is what his desired outcome looked like:

> 'As a result of this paper, I want two key board members, Fred Bloggs and Mary Smith, to AGREE to the business exploring ways to deepen existing customer relationships as the next growth strategy.'

The CMO felt that if he could address Mary and Fred's concerns, he would address the questions from other more supportive board members also.

Short List explained the benefits of two options before highlighting risks of pushing customer acquisition

The CMO did not shy away from his proposal in the main message. In this case, they wanted to prioritise the order the business addressed the options.

The CMO then supported it by discussing three potential ways of supporting growth without getting too deeply into each.

It offered a solid rationale for locking in existing customers two different ways without yet acquiring new customers.

In other situations, you may want support for investigating a set of options that will require you to prioritise the effort of doing so, likely at the expense of other tasks.

You can see the CMO's story on page 82.

The CMO provided the paper in prose format as a prelude to a rich discussion

The CMO went to this meeting well prepared, following extensive discussions with the CEO and the board chair. These discussions helped shape both the strategy for the board discussion and the substance of the paper. They also empowered the CEO and Chair to drip feed ideas into conversations with other board members in readiness for the meeting.

By workshopping the one-pager together, they felt confident they were ready to address Mary and Fred's questions.

As expected, the directors grilled them deeply on their reasons as to why the CMO did not recommend adopting all three paths simultaneously. The CMO convinced them during a lively debate that quality growth was an essential first priority. He was clear that he was also in favour of rapid growth, but only if it was sustainable.

The CMO left the meeting with support to deepen existing customer relationships as a first step. He also understood the board's

Offering a short list of options to explore

At our recent strategy day, we agreed to explore the most promising options for increasing revenue while not increasing customer churn.

We are now ready to outline three potential growth strategies for your consideration.

What strategies do you recommend that we explore?

We recommend exploring ways to serve existing customers better before accelerating customer acquisition.

Option 1: Increasing sales of existing products and features is a quick and promising way to lift revenue by X and cut churn by Y.	Option 2: Upgrading our support and maintenance package will lift revenues by Y and deepen customer relationships.	Option 3: Extending our customer base is risky until we are fully locked in with existing customers.
Broadening customer adoption of existing Mega 1 and Mega 2 features has potential to lift revenues by X. 1. Mega 1 and Mega 2 are only partially utilised by 80% of our customer base, with 50% of customers only using the finance features and few if any of the project management or human resource mgmt tools. 2. Extending existing Mega 1 and Mega 2 licenses to incorporate new features is financially appealing for clients and can materially increase our own margins. 3. 10 of our top 50 customers have indicated they are willing to explore our project management and finance features. Introducing minor products Mega 3 and Mega 4 to existing finance and technology customers has potential to further lift revenue by Z. Experience suggests that the more customers make use of our products, the harder it is for them to swap out to a competitor.	A larger and more highly skilled support team would help both lift sales and cut churn. They would: a. Identify opportunities for clients to extend their use of Mega 1 and Mega 2, and potentially also to adopt Mega 3 and Mega 4. b. Provide better service to our existing customers, reducing the potential for dissatisfaction and churn. Support packages can be designed competitively to encourage uptake and provide opportunities to learn more about customer needs that we can meet in the future. Competitor One has also neglected their support and maintenance business, potentially providing us with a competitive advantage if we improve ours.	1. 12 of our top 50 customers gave us a lower Net Promotor Score last quarter compared with the year before, indicating growing dissatisfaction with our post-sales service. 2. The current support team is stretched, with rising absenteeism since we signed our two largest deals last half. 3. Customer churn during the first three years significantly impacts our bottom line and our reputation. 4. The current sales pipeline is strong without further accelerating acquisition in the coming two years.

impatience and committed to return to the next meeting with a plan to accelerate efforts to strengthen relationships with existing customers.

This or That for explaining which option is best for capturing an opportunity or solving a problem

X is best for solving Y	We explored these	Option X is best	Do X

This or That is an even-handed structure that enables you to explain your preferred option against key criteria. Given many leadership groups request options analyses, this is a popular structure.

I hesitated in using a return-to-office example, but it is conceptually simple, contemporary and vexing for many organisations at the time of writing. Do they take Elon Musk's lead and insist everyone returns to the office full-time, or do they go the way of the likes of Atlassian, which countered with a 'work from home forever' offer to anyone from Tesla who did not want to return to the office?

Even if you are reading this well after the pandemic has dissipated and these issues are no longer as relevant, the story showcases the pattern well.

This story relates to a large wholesaler struggling with the emerging work-from-home culture. The SLT had been flexible for some time, in part because of their varied views on the subject. However, leaders felt that some employees were taking unfair advantage of the flexibility that working from home offers.

The CEO had raised the issue urgently at the most recent SLT meeting. He was tipped into action by two things.

A mid-level leader he had specifically asked to meet online with cameras on for a sensitive conversation had dialled in on their phone. When asked why, the executive said they were out running personal errands and would prefer to have an audio call.

Simultaneously, the employee satisfaction survey results were disappointing.

This combination led the CEO to ask the head of People and Culture to work out how to get more people in the office more of the time to increase his confidence in the organisation's culture. Here's the breakdown before I walk you through the story in more detail:

1. *Strategise:* To gain universal agreement from the SLT.
2. *Synthesise:* This or That set up a rich options discussion.
3. *Visualise:* The short PowerPoint supported a lengthy debate.

Here is how it played out.

The head of People and Culture was both delighted to be given this assignment and aware of the challenges. She had been working from the office almost full-time throughout the pandemic and thrived on the interaction with colleagues. She was keenly aware, though, that some of her SLT colleagues as well as pockets within the organisation felt quite the opposite. Some had even moved their families to country towns and had no plans to return to the city.

In thinking through her presentation, she decided that the Chief Technology Officer was core to success.

The CTO's engineering team was high-performing and loved working from home full-time. He was concerned they would be compelled to return to the office more often than he believed necessary to maintain that performance. He was also aware of the strong competition for engineering talent in the local market, where the likes of Atlassian offered a work from home guarantee.

So, she crafted an outcome statement like this:

'As a result of this presentation, I want the CTO to ACTIVELY SUPPORT the return-to-office strategies for the whole organisation and for his team.'

You will note that 'actively support' is not in the pattern picker framework. I chose to deviate from the basics to make a point with this example.

If the CTO is willing to actively support this strategy, he is willing to take many of the actions listed in the strategy section. He will have agreed to the strategy, approved it, changed his perspective, decided this is the way forward and endorsed it.

He is not just providing token support.

The end result will be that he will actively support the strategy by asking his mid-level leaders to 'nudge' most colleagues into the office two-plus days a week.

Carefully considering how far you can move someone in a specific interaction is essential in defining the response you will aim for in a specific communication.

This or That set up a rich options discussion

The head of People and Culture interviewed everyone on the SLT and held focus groups with a number of the mid-level managers across the organisation to be confident she understood the issues. She combined this with deep dives into research from the various human resources communities she was part of as well as informal discussion forums such as Quora and with peers in other organisations.

Many were facing the same challenge. How to get people back in the office while not losing critical team members?

She informally updated the SLT on her progress at their weekly meeting for a month while having informal discussions with each of them in parallel. A number of these conversations were feisty but productive, as colleagues came to see the flexibility she was planning.

Once her recommendation firmed in her mind, she tested her narrative with the CEO. Together they worked carefully through the potential objections from each SLT member and tweaked the recommendation accordingly. She then prepared a short presentation outlining her options analysis and recommendation.

You can see how it played out on page 86.

The short PowerPoint supported a lengthy debate

When the day came for the team meeting, the head felt confident she would get the necessary result, even though the CTO was only begrudgingly supportive.

The remaining members of the SLT were won over by the opportunity to allow some team members to continue working from home most of the time where personal circumstances dictated it.

The CTO was won over in the end by three things: he could 'nudge' rather than 'compel' his people to return to the office, he could tailor the in-office requirements to suit his team's specific needs and he could create exemptions where high-performing team members' personal circumstances merited it.

More on discussing options

This or That and Short List are not the only ways to discuss options even though they provide a useful platform. Depending on where you are up to in your options discussions, you can make strategic choices about your desired outcome, which in turn influences your pattern choice.

On page 87, I share an overview of a decision-making framework I use for large decisions. It outlines key project stages that may require different types of options discussions, each requiring fresh thinking about which pattern may suit.

You might, for example, merge deductive patterns together or follow a Make the Case pattern to explain criteria by criteria why your preferred option is best.

This or That explains which option is best and how to implement it

Leadership had hoped to continue running the business with most staff working from home four to five days per week. Recent employee satisfaction surveys have led the senior team to question their stance. Middle management has concerns about their ability to nurture junior team members, sustain a cohesive corporate culture and maintain productivity with such a high degree of remote working.

We have now completed our review as to the best way to increase the time employees spend in the office and are ready to make our recommendation.

What do you recommend?

We recommend asking mid-level leaders to 'nudge' most colleagues toward spending two-plus days per week in the office to lift culture and performance.

We explored a mix of options for increasing the time employees spend working from the office.	Mid-level leaders nudging most colleagues to spend two-plus days in the office each week is the best option.	So, let's help mid-level leaders to nudge their teams back into the office.

• We explored different approaches for lifting employee satisfaction while continuing to work from home full time, given many team members have a strong preference for working from home (list them).
• We explored ways to incentivise, or 'pull' colleagues to return to the office of their own accord to avoid the risk of being heavy-handed (list them).
• We explored a blend of leadership nudges (gentle pushes) and incentives to better balance employee rights and responsibilities (list them).
• We explored 'pushes' requiring 80+% return to the office for all head office employees to align with pre-COVID norms where many worked from home one day each week.
	• A balance of push and pull approaches is best.
	  ▪ Agreeing some 'push' mandates about minimum office times will increase the chance that team members return.
	  ▪ Relying solely on the soft 'pull' approach hasn't been effective here or at other organisations.
	• Mid-level leaders have the right balance of authority and proximity to drive this change.
	• Tailoring to roles and short-term individual circumstances will reduce the risk of turnover in a tight talent market where teams can demonstrate their ability to maintain high performance and a cohesive culture.
		Agree minimum in-office requirements while ensuring practicality.
		• Agree minimum for all head office teams, ideally 2 days per week, while allowing short- and longer-term exceptions where necessary.
		• Design the in-office schedule to suit team needs while not requiring extra seating (eg to avoid all hands on all teams making the same day their in-office day).
		• Communicate early so employees have enough notice to change personal arrangements.
		
		Monitor and manage to ensure compliance.
		• Report monthly for the coming quarter and quarterly after that until a new balance is restored.
		• Agree consequences for those who do not return to the office on the agreed minimum number of days.

Different ways to discuss options at key project stages

Alerting to a problem or opportunity	Deciding which options to explore	Recommending which option to implement	Agreeing the implementation plan	Implementing the solution
Potential outcomes, ie you need stakeholders to ..				
> Agree the problem or opportunity is big enough to warrant attention	> Agree that these are the right options to explore; or > Commit resources to conduct the options analysis	> Support your recommendation	> Agree with the implementation plan; or > Help implement the plan	> Agree with the proposal to adjust the current plan
Potential messages				
> Explain that this problem or opportunity warrants attention	> Offer up options to be considered; or > Explain the support and/or resources needed to conduct the options analysis	> How each option stacks up against evaluation criteria	> Different ways for implementing the recommended solution	> Offer different ways to adjust the plan; or > Offer different implementation strategies
Potential patterns				
> Make the Case to recommend assessing whether an opportunity or a problem warrants attention > Nugget to explain that something is a big opportunity or a big problem, without directly recommending action	> Short List to explain which options to consider with or without embedding a resource request within your reasoning > Make the Case or Top Up to justify a resource request	This or That or variations of other structures that allow you to embed options evaluation within your reasoning, eg • Golden • Make the Case • Oh Dear	This or That or variations of other structures that allow you to embed options evaluation within your reasoning, eg • Golden • Make the Case • Oh Dear	> Change Tack to suggest making a change to the plan > Nike to explain the plan without making a case for it > Top Up to explain why and how the plan needs improving

While this is a more sophisticated structuring strategy, you can experiment using the Pattern Picker to land the most suitable structure[7]. It helps you identify which pattern suits you best, before offering a PowerPoint download with specific instructions for your pattern.

Recommending improvements

Sometimes you don't need to go for something new, but rather need to improve what is already in play. I offer two patterns for doing this.

Change Tack is superb for building on previous success while Top Up is ideal for educating audiences about what is required for success.

Let's now take a look at each along with their case study.

Change Tack for addressing upcoming changes

Make a change to reach goal	We have progressed toward goal	Need to make a change to reach goal	Make a change

Change Tack is a wonderful pattern for project updates where good progress has been made, but a change is needed to help the team deliver the next stage. It offers an opportunity to engage the audience with good news before outlining

recommended changes. These changes may be in response to problems discovered in a project, opportunities for optimising results or external risks that have recently been identified.

I have chosen an example that we developed in one of my favourite (so far!) working sessions from my public program. The version I share is adapted from a post-mortem from the head of projects at a local government department. The three parts are as follows:

1. *Strategise:* To excite everyone about what had been achieved while tactfully recommending future improvements.
2. *Synthesise:* Change Tack warmed the leadership group before making some bold recommendations.
3. *Visualise:* The message was presented online to the top executives.

The strategy was to excite everyone while tactfully recommending future improvements

An experienced head of IT projects for a local government area had great visibility of the way the Cyber Response Program was implemented after a cyber attack. He also had deeper experience in managing incidents like this than the leadership.

---

7   ClarityFirstProgram.com/ClarityHub

This both offered opportunity and required delicacy lest he be seen to be a critic rather than wanting to help others to succeed. The critical risk to overcome for future incidents, however, lay in regularly changing instructions from the new and inexperienced Chief Technology Officer and other leadership team members.

To that end, his desired outcome read like this:

> 'As a result of this online presentation I want the executive leadership group to COMMIT to protecting the team from unnecessary challenges during future emergencies.'

Change Tack warmed the leadership group before making some bold recommendations

The head of projects felt strongly that the response had been a huge success and that the team needed to be recognised for their efforts. This was particularly acute as the new CTO was inexperienced and 'flip flopped' frequently on both the way to handle the incident and how to prioritise it in relation to other BAU activities.

Change Tack was the perfect choice given it highlighted key successes before offering suggestions for optimising future responses. We believed it kept the right balance between being respectful and being frank and fearless. Page 90 walks through the story.

The message was presented online to the top executive

The head of projects was offered 30 minutes for the post-mortem discussion. He rehearsed thoroughly before the meeting given his concerns about the new members of the leadership team not appreciating the need for tightening the response management.

He engaged the newly minted CTO before the meeting to be confident he supported his recommendations and agreed to share the spotlight in updating the executive group.

This enabled the project's head and the CTO to together help the new, non-technical leaders avoid being lulled into a false sense of security. The project's head believed it was important for them to know that the success rested on a number of people 'pulling all-nighters' to address the breach.

The meeting was a success thanks to deft collaboration between the projects head and the CTO during the meeting. They spent about 15 minutes talking through the story and the remainder of the call discussing the proposed plan.

Encouraging decision-makers to change tack

Implementing the Cyber Rescue Response (CRP) following the recent cyberattack has provided terrific lessons for us in managing difficult situations that we can leverage in the future.

Having now debriefed with the team, we want to share some lessons learned that will help us as senior leaders better prepare for future incidents.

What did you learn?

We can respond to future incidents even more smoothly if we refine the CRP to protect the team from last-minute changes.

We successfully delivered the CRP under huge challenges following the recent hacking attempt.	Despite this success, we can do more to protect the team from last-minute changes during future emergencies.	Let's refine the program.

• We were alerted to the breach within minutes of it occurring, highlighting the effectiveness of our recently upgraded monitoring systems.
• We notified critical stakeholders very quickly after the breach occurred:
  ▪ leadership within 30 minutes
  ▪ impacted customers within six hours via multiple channels
  ▪ regulators in parallel with customers.
• We identified and patched the vulnerability within 36 hours, with critical team members working through the night to deliver the fix.
• We worked together effectively with all relevant departments, including the newly appointed head of corporate affairs and the public relations agency.
	• Putting a Response Matrix in place would reduce the risk of derailing BAU projects that by necessity must be put on hold when the CRP is enacted.
	• Establishing a powerful Mission Control Team for future disasters to buffer the responders against left-field requests.
	• Strengthening leadership skills for everyone who needs to stay cool in stressful times:
	  ▪ learning to 'respond' rather than 'react' in times of challenge will lead to clearer more confident directions
	  ▪ empowering project members to directly engage decision-making bodies will improve mid-crisis prioritisation
	  ▪ encouraging leaders to ask questions before agreeing to make changes that could have detrimental impact.
		• Create a working group to develop a Response Matrix.
		• Agree roles and responsibilities for the Mission Control Team during future disasters.
		• See day-to-day situations as an opportunity to practise responding rather than reacting.
		• Provide opportunities for leaders and project members to role play difficult situations, including surprise drills.

Top Up to recommend improvements

Top up to succeed at Y	Succeeding at Y requires X	We must top up to succeed at Y	Top up

Top Up lays out a way to educate decision-makers about what is required for success. In an era of increasing technology complexity, this structure gets a good workout educating non-technical leaders about what is required for a tool or system to succeed.

This pattern is also a polite way to engage leaders who have designed systems that are now outdated – ie, to explain that although something may have worked in the past, the system is no longer fit for purpose.

In this instance, a technology company had expanded over the past two years to add consulting services to its offering. Given this diversification was successful, the leadership wanted to push for more rapid growth. They were also mindful, however, of the need to lay the right foundations before they did so.

This story outlines how the Chief Technology Officer sought permission from to upgrade the Enterprise Management System (EMS) to better support the larger, more complex business

Here's the high-level breakdown:

1. *Strategise:* To help non-technical board members appreciate how the EMS could support growth.

2. *Synthesise:* Top Up laid out the success criteria early.

3. *Visualise:* The message was delivered as a PowerPoint presentation to the board.

The strategy was to help non-technical board members appreciate how the EMS could support growth

Although this story was not contentious, the CTO was aware of the competition for funds, given every area was assessing their bench strength. He was facing two other challenges:

▶ He had recently been awarded an extra $3 million to strengthen other technology areas, so needed to make a strong case for this system upgrade. His peers may think he has 'had his turn'.

▶ Several powerful board members preferred investing in front-of-house systems over enterprise management tools. On introducing TopOps seven years prior, it had taken much persuasion to gain their support and they believed it still met their needs.

In light of this, the CTO's desired outcome went like this:

'As a result of this board meeting, I want the two "old-guard" board members to ENDORSE upgrading TopOps from Bronze to Gold.'

His felt that if he and the CEO convinced these two directors of the value of the EMS upgrade, they would carry the board. They were more confident of gaining agreement to upgrade an existing system than to migrate to a new one, which led them to avoid raising that possibility.

Top Up laid out the success criteria early

The CTO and CEO worked closely with the Chair to ensure their paper covered all extra issues that the senior team had not required. They felt that comparing the required functions and highlighting the gap between that and what was needed fo growth would be convincing.

Given two old-guard directors saw the growth agenda as part of their legacy and leadership support for the upgrade was so strong, they were confident in their messaging, laid out on page 93.

The message was delivered as a PowerPoint presentation to the board

The CTO prepared a detailed PowerPoint that unpacked the story. The board received it a week before the meeting to provide plenty of time for review.

Rather than engaging with the two directors themselves, the CTO and CEO liaised with the Chair, who then spoke with the directors. They preferred a low-key approach and were confident in the Chair's support for the recommendation.

The meeting went well, although both directors offered predictably strong challenge on the need to upgrade. The CTO effectively addressed their challenge, in part by pointing their proportionality. They were upgrading to Gold rather than Platinum and avoiding the extra costs of migrating to a whole new platform.

Now that we have looked at ways to use patterns as a quick-start to find and frame your message, let's look at firming up a message using first principles.

This next section will highlight the power of combining logic and synthesis to form a 'thinking machine' that helps us both create and test our message.

Persuading leaders to top up to deliver more value

At October's strategy day we agreed that DataCo would pursue an ambitious growth agenda, which depended upon first tightening several aspects of our operations. Each area agreed to identify opportunities to tighten their operations over the coming six months.

The technology team has now identified the priority area that needs strengthening to support the growth agenda.

What needs strengthening?

We recommend allocating up to $1.3m to upgrade TopOps from Bronze to Gold to support the faster service and greater customisation rapid growth will require.

Our growth agenda requires a powerful and affordable Enterprise Management System (EMS).	We need to upgrade our current Bronze TopOps package to Gold to underpin growth.	Therefore, we recommend upgrading our Top Ops package to Gold.
• It must support all key aspects of our business, including the to-be expanded support centre, core technology development teams, the complex project management needs of the rapidly growing consulting teams and other head office functions. • It must enable us to configure bespoke reports to accommodate the wide range of activities we undertake. • It must have a high reliability score with limited downtime and fast approachable customer services if needed. • It must be user-friendly, with smooth workflows across all areas to minimise time spent processing information from any location. • It must fit within the proposed $3m systems budget.	Our current Bronze package is underweight, re: both functionality and support. • It supports most support centre requirements except its project management toolkit, which is 'light'. • The current reports lack features needed by the new client-service team and are clunky to create, slow to generate. • Although problems are rare, TopOps can be down for up to seven days before complex issues, including at times the cashflow critical invoicing capability, are resolved under a Bronze-level support package. The Gold package offers the extra features we need without using the full systems budget or requiring a major change management effort. • It includes stronger project management tools including more complex reports needed by our client-service team. • It offers a more personalised support package to reduce risk of downtime. • It fits within our current $3m systems budget given we only spend $1.5m on the Bronze Package.	Confirm Mary as project manager as soon as Project Giraffe finishes next month. Develop an upgrade plan with clear deliverables. • Agree how much of the plan can be delivered with BAU resources and how many full-time equivalent resources we need as well as contractors for each aspect of the work. • Decide project time frames. • Deliver proposed plan and deliverables to SLT for review by xx date. Allocate $1m to $1.3m in the coming FY systems budget to upgrade TopOps to Gold. • Budget $300K extra annually to upgrade to a Gold-level license. • Budget $700K to configure the reporting capability to cater for operational needs. • Allow for contingencies that Mary may identify when she develops formal the upgrade plan.

CHAPTER 5

Firm up your message by iterating around a one-page message map

Message maps are the engine-room of this approach. They help us arrange our information into a tight structure that showcases the main message and the logic behind it.

They begin with a short introduction that primes an audience to be ready for our single, insightful main message. We then support that main message by organising our information logically.

Easy, right?

Superficially yes, but practically no.

Visualising your ideas into a hierarchy as below is hugely powerful. By understanding specifically how the

ideas relate to each other in both the one-page message map and the final communication is key. Ensuring each idea tightly connects to the others is where the power lies.

I now explain how to power up your own communication. I encourage you to

▶ Lean on structure to lift the quality of your messaging.

▶ SCORE the quality of your messaging.

▶ Review an example to see the difference between strong and weak.

Let's dive in to each of these one by one.

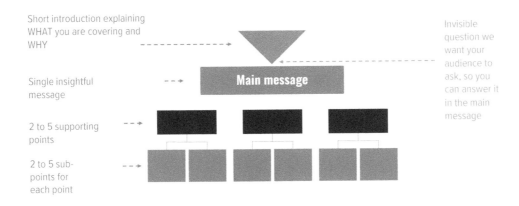

Short introduction explaining WHAT you are covering and WHY

Invisible question we want your audience to ask, so you can answer it in the main message

Single insightful message

Main message

2 to 5 supporting points

2 to 5 sub-points for each point

▶ Lean on structure to lift the quality of your messaging

In this I break the structure into parts to help you create and evaluate each one.

I explain how the introduction quickly draws your audience toward your main message. It avoids offering lots of history and background, but rather readies your audience for your single, overarching and insightful point of view.

I then offer four different levels of 'idea' so you can decide how much value your main message needs to deliver.

Lastly, I explain how to structure the supporting points two ways to round out that message and prepare a paper or presentation that is both clear and compelling. Let's dig in.

The introduction quickly draws your audience toward your main message

Many papers and presentations offer too much background before getting to the main point. I see many offer details that they think the audience needs to know in order to understand their main point.

I challenge that idea, and instead encourage you to quickly arrive at the main message. If you worry that some audience members don't know as much about the topic as others, shift the

background to pre-meetings, link to past papers and use the appendix. This avoids punishing those who are on top of the material and makes it easier for everyone to get to the heart of the matter. It will also help you cull unnecessary content.

I'll now walk through the three-parts of the introduction, offering visual clues like the one below to help you keep track of where we are up to in the overall structure.

This first navigator highlights the inverted triangle at the top of the structure, which refers to the introduction.

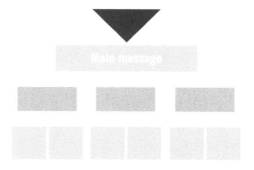

The introduction draws your audience toward your main message. Contrary to common practice, it is short – ideally no more than 15 per cent of the total document length. I begin by using a super simple camping example to explain how the three components of the introduction engage your audience in your topic.

Begin by explaining what you are discussing

If you have worked in consulting, you may have heard this first element described as 'the situation'.[8]

I prefer to describe this element simply as 'what we are discussing'. It is typically a short sentence or two that lets your audience know which mutually relevant topic you are introducing.

It will most likely introduce a known problem or opportunity, or share an observation about a familiar situation. It should also be timely, topical and tight. Timely in that it covers recent information that should be familiar to the audience, topical in that it introduces the relevant topic for discussion and tight in that it is short!

This short section simply engages them in the issue. It helps them shift their mind from where it was to where you want it to be.

Make it relevant by explaining why you are discussing that topic now

Once your audience knows what you want to discuss, they will naturally want to know why that topic is relevant now. The diagram on the next page illustrates what happens inside our audience's heads as they read or listen to us speak.

I recommend using no more than two sentences to explain very simply why you are communicating with them now about the topic you have just introduced. It may be that you have a recommendation for them to consider, a request, an update or perhaps you need their help.

You may be able to make it more interesting than that, but it must point directly toward your main message.

Prime your audience to ask a question

Once your audience understands what you are discussing and why you are discussing it, they will naturally ask one, single obvious question that you can then answer with the main message.

This question might be something simple, such as 'What is your recommendation?', or perhaps, "How should we proceed?" Although this question rarely goes into your document, writing it on your message map focuses you on guiding your audience toward your main message. It also confirms for you the single, highest-order question you want to answer.

---

8   Although Barbara Minto recommends keeping this section really short, some consultants use this element differently. I commonly see the 'situation' become a lengthy description of the background rather than being used how it was originally intended.

Imagine, for example, if we were good friends and I said something like, 'The other day we talked about going away for a weekend'. You might then wonder, Why is my friend saying that? I would then naturally say, 'I have an idea', which would in turn lead you to wonder what my idea is.

Notice that in offering the thought 'I have an idea' I am not giving my answer away just yet, but I am priming my friend to be ready to hear what that idea, or main message, is.

This illustrates what can happen at the start of a paper or presentation. Explaining what you are discussing and why readies your audience for your main message, no matter how simple or complex the message, as below.

Distil your whole story into one single, insightful main message

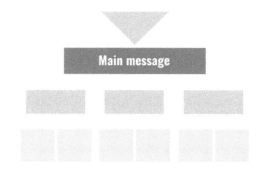

At 25 words or less, your main message is short, contains one single idea and packs a punch. It should be so relevant and powerful that your audience's response is 'Wow, that's useful', or 'Wow, that's insightful'.

WHAT – The other day we talked about going away for a weekend.

Why are you reminding me about that?

WHY – I have an idea of what we might do.

What is your idea?

MAIN MESSAGE – It would be fun to go camping.

COMMUNICATOR
DRAWING AUDIENCE IN TO THE TOPIC

AUDIENCE
ASKING 'INVISIBLE QUESTIONS'

This main message is not a list of ideas strung together, but one single thought that captures the essence of the story.

It may summarise by describing what the data says, or synthesise to explain what the data means. Synthesis ties the facts to the situation, offering a clear point of view.

Offering this single, insightful message early in your communication will make your audience curious. The more insightful it is, the more curious they will be.

My value ladder below calibrates the difference between lower-value 'information' and more valuable ideas, or 'insights'. The difference is synthesis.

1. *Insight:* We recommend investing $2.4m next year to implement four stand-alone initiatives so we can meet our ambitious objectives. *(Ideally this.)*
2. *Recommendation:* We recommend investing $2.4m to implement four stand-alone initiatives next year that will realign our IT and business strategies. *(Possibly this.)*
3. *Implication:* We identified six strategic themes that may impact our strategy. *(Possibly useful when updating your manager on your early stage findings.)*
4. *Information:* We identified six strategy themes. *(Unlikely this unless a junior researcher.)*

Not all messages deliver the same insight or VALUE ...

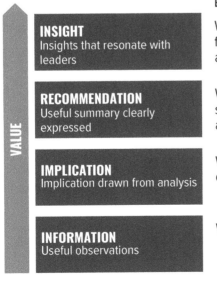

VALUE

INSIGHT
Insights that resonate with leaders

RECOMMENDATION
Useful summary clearly expressed

IMPLICATION
Implication drawn from analysis

INFORMATION
Useful observations

EXAMPLES

We recommend investing $2.4m next year to implement four stand-alone initiatives that help us meet our ambitious objectives.

We recommend investing $2.4m to implement four stand-alone initiatives next year and realign our IT and business strategies.

We identified six strategic themes that may impact our strategy.

Why is that relevant?

We identified six strategy themes.

Organise the ideas in a well-structured hierarchy

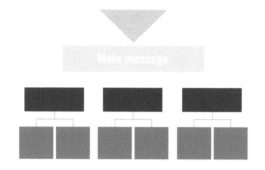

I use one of two frames to arrange supporting ideas. Both act like a 'thinking machine' that pushes you to think harder to articulate a clear and insightful point of view. They use logic and synthesis to help you clarify and convey your messaging so it is easy for your audience to grasp quickly.[9]

I first share why I think these two ways of structuring your ideas suit business communication better than some others before explaining how they work.

Grouping and deductive structures come into their own for engaging busy leaders

I realise the idea of using just two structures might seem confining. It certainly did when I began using structured thinking in my early days at McKinsey. I had previously learned from authors and journalists who were all excellent communicators and wonderful teachers. They were experts in their genre.

When at teachers' college, I learned creative writing from Mem Fox, one of Australia's top children's authors, who shared wonderful techniques for writing creatively to entertain. (Her books, such as *Possum Magic* and *Wilfrid Gordon McDonald Partridge*, are magical.)

The creative writing techniques that Mem taught were, however, singly unsuited to untangling a 50-page finance deck, or to clarify and convey the top line of a complex narrative.

The journalism techniques I learned at university were also of limited help. These were perfectly suited to writing news articles which called out a snappy headline. But they did not structure a message so that a time-poor audience could quickly find and unpick the logic behind the author's point of view. The headline idea was easy to find, but the reader must read to the end to find the underlying logic.

Other literary narrative structures suggest building the tension toward the big reveal. Holding your audience on that journey

---

9   William Minto first described using logic to communicate in *Logic: Inductive and Deductive*. Barbara Minto also discussed combining logic and synthesis to structure your messaging in *The Minto Pyramid Principle*.

requires great skill and, in my experience, creates great risk that you lose them on the way. The audience is also required to read to the end to find what they need, which senior audiences dislike.

I do want to assure you, however, that using grouping and deductive structures does not mean staying away from more sophisticated communication techniques altogether. You and your team can most certainly use them when necessary. You can add analogy and imagery when you need to entertain, perhaps when delivering a keynote speech.

For now, I will focus on helping you and your team crystallise messaging that will engage your decision-makers and drive the progress you need. Once you and your team have mastered this, feel free to become more creative and layer on sophisticated entertainment techniques.

Grouping and deductive structures are powerful thinking machines

I now offer a bird's-eye view of both grouping and deductive structures to help you see which structure has been used and, broadly, whether the structure is in good shape or not. As you can see, they look different and serve different purposes.

Grouping: For almost any type of message supported by individual ideas

Grouping structures are both tightly structured and enormously flexible, suiting almost any kind of communication. They support the main message with a list of two to five independent yet tightly connected ideas.

Deductive: For recommendations supported by chained reasons and an action

Deductive structures offer a powerful way to outline a recommendation when you must build the case for it and explain how to deliver it in the same communication. They offer three points, the first two outlining the reasons why your recommendation is strong before the final point explains how to implement it.

To put some meat on that, I'll first explain how grouping structures work, using a simple camping example. Then I will do the same for deductive structures before moving to more complex professional material.

Grouping structures consist of two to five points that support any kind of message

Groupings suit action plans, business cases, recommendations, requests, research findings, updates – anything.

The magic lies in five rules. These rules enable us to test that we have organised our ideas to offer a clear, compelling and cohesive point of view. Let me quickly outline them before exploring each one. Each idea must be:

▶ A single idea expressed as a full sentence.

▶ One of two to five ideas at that level.

▶ Closely related to the idea at the level above in the hierarchy.

▶ Ordered logically relative to its peers.

▶ Distinct and essential to conveying a cohesive point of view.

Each point must be a single idea expressed as a full sentence

This pushes you to clarify your thinking. Relying on dot points, words or phrases alone leads to unfinished thinking and sloppy communication. Let me illustrate.

Version 1 is a quick note:
Park Access Pass

Version 2 is a complete sentence:
Go online before Thursday to buy the Cougar Mountain Park Access Pass so we have permission to camp there.

The full sentence cannot be misconstrued and is easier to position within the message map. In contrast, the rough note is not complete, and so is easier to misconstrue and misplace.

Each point must be one of two to five at that level

I often hear people say you should have three points. While it's true that great speeches often anchor around three, it is not wise to force your thinking into three grouped ideas. This can force ideas into unnatural relationships, which in turn obscures or distorts the message.

Finding genuine and insightful connections between ideas is how we generate greater clarity and insight while also enabling us to sort ideas into a hierarchy. So, why these limits?

Two is the smallest number of ideas you can group. One idea on its own is not a group; it's just a single idea. When I see a single bullet point or a 'list of one' I ask myself whether that point is really a couple of ideas jammed into one or if it actually is a single idea.

If it really is a single idea, and there are no other obviously missing 'companion ideas', I merge it with the idea above.

Here's an example. The original section went as follows:

> *We need to book for our upcoming trip.*
> - *Camping site*

In this case I merged the two points into a single point like this:

> *We need to book a camping site for our upcoming trip.*

This is more cohesive and requires less brain strain from the reader.

More than five ideas indicates more thinking is needed. Sometimes you can get away with a list of six ideas, but it is rarely necessary. Long lists point to incomplete thinking. The connections between the ideas have not been sufficiently clarified.

To address this, look closely at the relationships between the ideas. Find what they have in common and group them.

The example in the column to the right has six dot points organised into three sections. The three mid-level messages add materially to the synthesis and resulting clarity, making the narrative easier to follow.

Each point must be closely related to the idea at the level above in the hierarchy

A concept I call the Power of One is the simplest way to understand this.

This concept is that *one* idea leads to *one* 'invisible' question from the audience, which leads to *one* type of response. This helps you clarify whether the ideas really do belong together and whether it looks like they do. So, I ask two sub-questions.

Firstly, do the ideas belong together?

By that I mean that if the idea primes your audience to ask 'why is that true?', respond with reasons. For example, if I were to explain why camping would be the best getaway I could say something like this:

> *Main message: It would be fun to go camping at Cougar Mountain this weekend. Here's why:*
> 1. Cougar Mountain Park is great
>   - There is lots to do
>   - The area is beautiful and peaceful
> 2. You need a break
>   - You have been working too much
>   - You have time now your project is finished
> 3. I'll organise everything
>   - I have all the gear
>   - I know a great camping spot

This is persuasive in part because the ideas are relevant and well organised.

In contrast, mixing reasons, actions, criteria and facts is not only confusing, it is not persuasive.

In this next example you will see a confusing disconnect.

Main message: It would be fun to go camping this weekend.

1. Make the booking
   - Book accommodation
   - Book park pass
2. Camping is fun
   - You work too much
   - Reschedule your commitments
3. Prepare your gear
   - Check you have the gear you need
   - Pack your bag

This will frustrate my friend who likes camping and wants to know *how to make it happen*.

It is not clear whether you think the person you are speaking to likes camping or not. The first and third points are actions, explaining how to go camping. The middle point is a reason.

Identifying and fixing these disconnects clarifies the messaging, making more useful for you and your audience. It is also much easier to find such errors when drawing the ideas into a hierarchy (as below) than when reviewing a fully drafted paper or presentation.

Secondly, are the ideas in each group expressed as though they match each other?

We can help our audience grasp our message more easily if we make it obvious that our ideas belong together.

I call using the same language pattern for each point in a list being 'parallel'. For example, these two ideas belong together but are not expressed as though they do:

- Gear is ready
- Pack your bag

Making them both actions, and parallel, increases clarity for you and your friend:

- Check your gear is ready
- Pack your bag

Being parallel is a terrific discipline because it helps flush out whether ideas really do belong together and then show the audience that they do.

Once you have clarified that the ideas not only belong together, but look like they do, you will want to decide how to order them within each group.

Each idea must be ordered logically relative to peers

I use two methods to organise grouped ideas within a communication: sequence and scale.

I most commonly sequence actions. This means placing actions in the order in which they need to be tackled. This might mean an audience member needs to take five steps to complete a task or perhaps to understand Part 1 before they can appreciate Part 2. It may also mean tackling the most important items first.

Scale is the simplest way to arrange ideas that are not ordered by time. To order ideas by scale, I identify the theme and then usually work from largest to smallest. This might mean offering my reluctant camping friend the most enticing idea first and working toward less enticing ideas.

In this case my theme is defined as what I think my friend will find enticing. Note that there may be a difference between what I find enticing and what they find enticing.

In other situations, I might begin with quick wins or small issues first to get them out of the way before introducing the major points.

The key is to use a deliberate order, which was lacking in the confused camping example to the left.

This helps further crystallise our insights while also making it easier for the audience to follow.

Each point must be distinct and essential to conveying a cohesive point of view

This is where experience and judgment are essential in evaluating the quality of thinking in a communication. Confirming that ideas are distinct and separate is typically not so difficult.

However, confirming that each idea is not only essential, but that the ideas together form a cohesive point of view can be phenomenally difficult.

Consultants use an acronym for this process which I will adopt here for the sake of potential familiarity and alignment.

That acronym is MECE, said Meee Seee. Some firms simplify it to NONG, which embodies some Australia humour which I love and will explain shortly.

I'll unpack it in three parts to help you use it effectively when thinking through your own messaging.

MECE stands for 'Mutually Exclusive, Collectively Exhaustive'

Before exploring the concept further, let me define it for you.

▶ *Mutually exclusive:* This test isn't so hard. It asks whether the ideas are distinct, ie separate, and don't overlap each other. Once you have ordered the ideas by

sequence or scale, it should be fairly straightforward to resolve any gaps or overlaps, so long as each point is clearly articulated as a full sentence.

When I see clients use a phrase or a couple of key words my antenna goes up as this is where gaps and overlaps flourish.

▶ *Collectively exhaustive:* This one is harder. It asks you to assess whether the overall narrative is complete. Have you included all the ideas necessary to achieve your desired outcome?

There are two parts to this: one easier than the other.

First, have you included all of the ideas needed to support your main message? Have you covered all of the relevant issues required to support the main message as you have crafted it?

Secondly, double check whether this main message is actually sufficient. Have you posed the right question? For example, does your audience actually understand why your recommendation is solid and so only needs actions? Or, do they need to know why my recommendation matters? This can require quite a deal of judgement.

MECE allows topics to be discussed multiple times, so long as the message is distinct each time

In applying MECE, clients commonly confuse repeating topics with repeating ideas. By necessity, some topics, for example criteria for solving a problem, must be discussed multiple times within one communication.

The solution is to draft each point as a full sentence. This pushes you to say something about the criteria, not just to jot the name of the criteria down.

It is common, for example, to explain why one option is better than others. If so, you will describe how each option stacks up against each criterion. Each time you reference a criterion, you discuss it in relation to a different option.

In doing so you mention each criterion multiple times throughout the story, but in the context of a different idea.

I'll now come back to our camping example.

I'll lead with the main message and then offer two reasons that explain why one option is better than the other.

Each reason comments on the key decision-making criteria: cost, proximity to nature and comfort.

Main message: Camping would be a more fun and affordable way to soak in nature this weekend. Here's why:

1. Camping is less expensive and closer to nature than staying in an Airbnb, although admittedly less comfortable.
2. Staying at an Airbnb is more comfortable but also more expensive than camping and removes us from nature.

Each criterion is discussed against each option in a way that is relevant to that option.

MECE is a serious tool, yet can benefit from a bit of levity

Given MECE is used so widely in consulting, I am sticking with that. I do, however, like a simpler term: NONG. This stands for 'no overlaps, no gaps'. I like the irony of this. In Australian slang, 'nong' is short for 'ning nong', which is an insult used to describe a fool.

MECE – or NONG – is a deceptively simple test that can be very hard to get right. Those who master it are most definitely not fools.

Having now discussed how to group ideas, I'll offer a more detailed one-pager that pulls the key ideas together. I'll then move to deductive structures.

Visualising a grouping structure as a one-page message map

	A single insightful message that is 25 words or less and summarises or ideally synthesises your whole story.		

A short introduction that lets your audience know what you are discussing. It should include information that is familiar to the audience and bring their minds to a recent relevant event.

Most likely a single sentence that explains why you want to discuss the topic outlined above with your audience now.

The question you want to answer, which your audience will naturally want to ask after they have heard or read the context and trigger.

The single question your audience will naturally want to ask after learning your single message.

Point 1: The first of 2 to 5 points that responds to the same question your audience will naturally ask after hearing or reading the main message.	Point 2: The second of 2 to 5 points that responds to the same question the audience will naturally ask after hearing or reading the main message.	Points 3 to 5: More 'parallel' points if needed to further support the main message.
• The first of 2 to 5 sub-points that form either a grouping or deductive structure to elaborate on the top line point. • The second sub-point that follows the first, adopting either a grouping or deductive structure. • The third and subsequent sub-points, if necessary.	• As for point 1.	• As for point 1.

Deductive structures suit powerful recommendations

As for grouping structures, each point in a deductive chain needs to be a single, well-formed idea that synthesises or summarises the ideas below. The ideas are arranged differently, however.

In groupings, the two to five supporting points 'match' each other. In a deductive structure the three points are deliberately different. The first two set up the third.

Effective deductive structures follow three key rules. Each point:

1. Has a specific role to play as a statement, comment or recommendation.
2. Must closely relate to the other two without overlapping.
3. Over arches a tightly knit grouping structure.

Let's unpack each of those further.

Each point has a specific role to play as a statement, comment or recommendation

The first two supporting points, the statement and comment, together persuade your audience why your recommendation is right. The idea is that by the time you have run through the first two sections your audience is persuaded and ready to hear how to implement your recommendation:

▶ The *statement* introduces an issue that is news to your audience and sets the broad parameters for the rest of your recommendation. You might call it your 'major statement' or your 'thesis' if you are harking back to any logic study that you have undertaken.

▶ The *comment* narrows the discussion to focus on one part of the statement. Some might call this a 'minor statement' or in some settings the 'anti-thesis'. It starts with 'However', or a similar connecting word.

▶ The *recommendation, or 'therefore'*, explains first what you recommend so you can then explain how to implement it. This is supported by your implementation plan.

Each point must closely relate to the other two without overlapping

The statement, comment and recommendation must be connected super tightly but not overlap. This is true when a deductive chain appears at the top line or lower down in the supporting structure.

I like to colour-code the points to test I have the flow right. You can see in the next camping example that I have one part of the statement and the matching part of the comment yellow, and then one part of the comment blue along with the corresponding part in the recommendation.

You can also see that each of the colour-coded ideas in the supporting points mirrors concepts in the main message.

Each point must over arch a tightly knit grouping structure

Mapping the ideas visually helps you focus on the relationships between the ideas.

You can see from the colour-coded example above that each of the three top-line points sits above a grouped list. The same story in prose format looks like this:

> *Main message: Camping would be the most fun thing to do this weekend.*

This high-level message ties all of the supporting points together.

Statement: We could do lots of things this weekend (a new idea that is broad and sits above evidence, as below)

- Watching movies would be chill
- Eating out would be social
- Camping would be refreshing

Comment: But, camping is the most fun thing to do (comments on the statement, which sits above evidence, expressed as reasons or evidence, as below)

- Camping is more fun than the other options
- We want to get out of town
- We can afford it

Recommendation: So, let's camp! (recommends the now obvious way forward before setting up the implementation plan, as below)

- Make the booking
- Change other plans
- Pack your gear

If you look closely at the supporting points for each of the three top-line points in the deductive chain, you can see that patterns again come into play.

The first two points are both supported by a mini Nugget pattern. Both points are supported by evidence. The third point, the recommendation, is supported by a Nike pattern, ie a list of actions.

Below I offer a more detailed one-pager so you can see clearly the relationships between the ideas in a deductive structure.

I hope this reinforces the value of visualising your ideas, too, rather than just jotting down a list of bullet points.

Visualising a deductive structure as a one-page message map

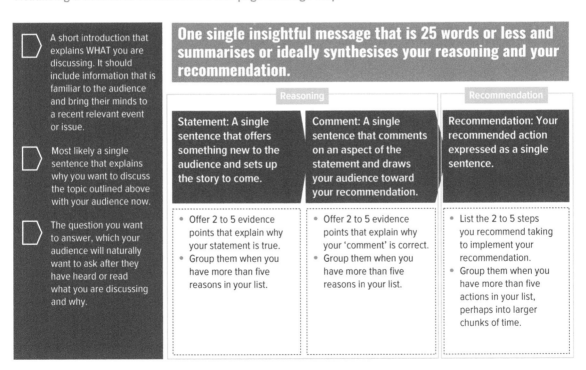

▶ SCORE the quality of your messaging

Now your ideas are sketched out as a message map, you want to test that they are strong. You want confidence that you are presenting a cohesive and compelling narrative that will help you deliver on your outcome.

This is where understanding the relationships between the ideas in your structure can help draw out the insights buried inside your own head and your team's heads also.

Over decades of being an outsider, I have learned that the structure itself can help find strengths and weaknesses in the messaging. It can lift you out of the detail to surface the insightful and impactful story you need to tell.

This has, in turn, led me by necessity to develop a fast technique for reviewing drafts.

I share my Scan, Score, Share technique with you here, so you can also benefit. I'll first explain how:

▶ Teaching lawyers turned my weakness into strength.
▶ Trusting the quality of the structure is a proxy for the quality of the thinking, and
▶ Working from the high-level messaging into the detail is fast and effective.

Teaching lawyers turned weakness into strength

In developing Scan, Score, Share, my weakness became my strength – and I hope it can for you too.

You might imagine my nerves when starting to teach lawyers how to write legal advice. Legal advice must be watertight. It's complicated, often convoluted and, regardless how well it's written, requires concentration to the very end. It is also rarely easy to read.

And lawyers are not only smart but also have a finely tuned appetite and ability for debate. This makes them good at their job. They would 'litigate' any suggestions I had – in part for fun and in part so they understood why and how they should tip their ideas about communication on their heads.

They were taught to first explain how they arrived at their insight. This was tricky as I recommend doing the opposite.

To top that, I needed to provide fast feedback on material I knew very little about to people who would quickly find fault.

How on earth? I relied on the only tool I had: structure.

Trusting the quality of the structure as a proxy for the quality of the thinking

I learned to trust that the structure, or shape, of the advice highlighted strengths and weaknesses in the quality of the thinking. This enabled me to find substantial problems within seconds without reading much, if anything, of the text. That might seem like a peculiar idea, so let me offer an analogy.

Imagine you are walking down the street to grab a coffee from your local café. As you stroll along you see the neighbour's dog. As usual, Fido has two ears, four legs and a tail. You barely notice the dog at all, unless of course you are friends and stop and give it a pat. You likely just think, *There goes Fido*.

If, however, one day you see that Fido is limping, you're likely to notice the limp more than anything else. Even if Fido were not familiar to you, you would notice the limp more than other features. The limp stands out in a way that the healthy dog does not. It might even make you sad as you wonder how it happened.

I realise your communication is more abstract and complex than Fido, but I want to illustrate the power of familiar shapes. For me, reviewing the legal advice became

a bit like finding Fido's limp. The message map became 'healthy Fido', and the breaks in the structure a bit like a limp.

In scanning for structural misalignment, I would quickly see if everything was in good shape, or not. When I spotted misalignment, I could zero in to unpick what was happening at that point. This enabled me to provide fast feedback to my clients.

So, let's set you up to review your own communication quickly and provide your team with fast feedback too.

Working from the high-level messaging into the detail is fast and effective

Working visually using a one-pager makes it easy to focus on the thinking that underpins communication and avoid getting lost in the details. You're not required to go on a time-consuming Easter egg hunt to find the insights.

The insights pop to the surface of the message map so you can scan and spot misalignment quickly – sometimes in seconds.

You can go through three steps to make that work. First, scan the message map to spot problems. Then, review more closely to score the communication against my SCORE framework. Finally, apply changes as needed or share your observations with the author.

I will now take you through these three steps one by one.

SCAN the message map to find thinking problems before reading (almost) anything

Now is a good time to remember Fido. Without wanting to over-stretch the analogy, imagine you have just seen Fido and without realising it you are checking to see if he's OK. Does he look happy? Well? Without any inkling that something might be wrong, you don't want to offer a full veterinary-grade checkup. You only want to take a quick look.

So, as with Fido, when reviewing the message map, start with the overall picture and then, after your preliminary view, you can dive deeper if you need to.

To explain how this works, I'll work from the general to the specific. I'll explain how I review the basic shape, section by section, before 'scoring' the communication during a deeper review.

So let's start our scan at beginning of the communication. Here's what I look for.

The introduction quickly draws your audience toward your main message

The introduction is short and includes three parts that together quickly draw your audience toward your main message. It does not provide screeds of background.

I look very quickly at the shape of these three introductory elements without reading them. Here's what I look for:

1. The *What* should be short. If it is bulging, you (or the author) has either explained new material or provided too much unnecessary background. Given an introduction should only contain timely material that should be known to the audience, this is a red flag. Elaboration is not needed, just a reminder.

2. The *Why* should be very, very short. If it is more than two sentences, you have a problem. The reason for communicating should be simple and short.

3. The *invisible audience question* should be so simple and obvious you think it's silly. The point of the 'what' and 'why' is to set up the audience to ask this question without even realising it. For now, just check that it looks short and simple.

The main message conveys the single most important idea in your communication

The main message should be one single sentence that is 25 words or less. If you have more than one sentence, you have a problem. If the box is bulging, you have a problem. If just a few words are in the box, you also have a problem. In all cases, synthesis is lacking.

Now is time to take a quick look at the shape of the supporting structure.

The structure backs up that message clearly and insightfully

The top-line structure sits right below the main message in our structure. It should include two to five top-line supporting points. If you only have one, or if you have more than five, you have a problem. If you have more than three points that include more than one starting with 'but' or 'however', you have a problem.

The supporting points should consist of two to five points in each list, with no more than one 'but' or 'however' in a deductive chain.

Using this framework, I can spot major structural problems in seconds. Although I typically register a few of the key words, I read almost nothing in this initial scan.

If you trust the structure to work, you will be able to do so too.

Without even reading the words on the page, we have a crude sense of how well thought through the ideas are, and can spot some high-level areas for improvement.

SCORE the structure to diagnose substantive issues

Now we have an inkling as to whether Fido is in good shape, or whether he has a limp.

Let's diagnose what is going on. If limping, it's time to ask whether Fido hurt himself badly or simply has a minor sprain. And, although not wanting to think in the negative is tempting, doing so is the fastest way to find and fix substantive issues in your or your team's message map.

This is the hardest step for at least two reasons: it requires a decent understanding of message map 'mechanics', and it can be very tempting to fix each problem as soon as you find it. However, I urge caution. Stay out of the detail just yet, lean further into the structure and focus on correcting the thinking before rewriting.

I offer my SCORE framework now to help diagnose deeper strengths and weaknesses.

SCORE is scalable

Sometimes this summary of the SCORE framework will be sufficient to guide your review.

It asks if the one-pager provides quality content in a quality way by asking if it meets five key criteria. It asks whether it ...

▶ *Sets* the scene quickly by drawing the audience toward one insightful message (Are the what, why and main message strong?).

▶ *Conveys* the right balance of strategic and operational detail (Are strategy and materiality appropriately catered for?).

▶ *Organises* the ideas in a well-structured hierarchy (Is the structure strong using grouping, deductive and MECE techniques?).

▶ *Readies* the audience quickly to achieve a quality outcome (Is it relevant and readable?).

▶ *Engages* the audience using a medium, style and tone that suits them (Is the communication skimmable and visual?).

You can download the summary below in the PowerPoint planner[8] so you have it close by when reviewing your team's communication.

---

8   ClarityFirstProgram.com/ClarityHub

SCORE framework summary

S	C	O	R	E
Sets the scene **quickly by drawing the audience toward one insightful message**	Conveys the right **balance of strategic and operational detail**	Organises the ideas **in a well-structured hierarchy**	Readies the audience **for a productive discussion**	Engages the audience **using a medium, style and tone that suits them**
What Why Main Message	Strategy Materiality	Grouping Deductive MECE	Relevant Readable	Skimmable Visual

SCORE is comprehensive

Let's now 'double click' on each element. I imagine you will want to go more deeply into these for more significant communication so offer a complete list here for reference.

I ask whether the communication does the following. Does it ...

S – Set the scene quickly by drawing the audience toward one insightful message by ...

1. Explaining **WHAT** is being discussed early:
   a. Quickly reminding the audience about the familiar problem, opportunity or observation the paper will discuss
   b. Introducing that topic in a way that is timely and tight

2. Explaining **WHY** this topic is being discussed now

3. Offering **one insightful and visible main message** that unifies the whole paper in 25 words or less

C – Convey the right balance of strategic and operational detail by ...

4. Positioning the story appropriately in relation to strategy

5. Aligning with the right materiality thresholds for this audience

O – Organise the ideas in a well-structured hierarchy by ...

6. Aligning ideas at every level of a grouping structure four ways:
   a. Number: Each group has two to five ideas
   b. Type: Each idea is the same kind of idea as its peers
   c. Vertically: Each idea answers the single natural question prompted by the idea above
   d. Horizontally: Ideas are arranged logically, likely by sequence or scale

7. Ensuring the top-line ideas in a deductive structure each play their specific role, ie
   a. The statement anchors the narrative around one substantive idea that is both new to the audience and broader in scope than the comment
   b. The comment narrows the discussion to focus on one key concept that was introduced in the statement
   c. The statement and comment are so persuasive that together they prepare your audience for your recommendation, so it does not come as a surprise

8. *Supporting the top-line of a deductive structure well, which means that:*

   a. Both the statement and comment are supported by tightly grouped ideas

   b. The recommendation ('therefore') is supported by tightly grouped actions

9. *Avoiding gaps and overlaps, ie, the ideas are MECE (Mutually Exclusive, Collectively Exhaustive).* This involves:

   a. Categorising and labeling ideas correctly

   b. Avoiding ideas overlapping each other

   c. Leaving nothing out

R – Ready the audience for a productive discussion by ...

10. *Focusing only on matters relevant to the desired outcome*

11. *Being easily readable, using language that is active and parallel throughout, ie by:*

   a. Synthesising or summarising ideas at every level into fully formed sentences that the audience will find insightful, ie useful, impactful and interesting

   b. Expressing ideas clearly, so the audience doesn't need to ask for clarification.

   c. Using parallel language so the ideas obviously match each other

---

10 ClarityFirstProgram.com/ClarityHub

E – Engage the audience using a medium, style and tone that suits them by ...

12. *Formatting ideas so it is easy to skim the hierarchy of the messaging, in any medium*

13. *Using simple images, charts and diagrams to help the audience quickly grasp ideas*

Make sure you download the summary along with the associated scoring rubric before your one-month free access Clarity Hub[10] expires if you have not yet done so.

Before practising this process on an example, I'll give you some ideas for sharing your observations with your team.

SHARE your insights in the most suitable way

Here are some thoughts to help iterate the messaging before preparing the final document:

▶ Share the SCORE framework with your team before you ask them to prepare a draft. This way they will know what you are using to review their messaging.

▶ Begin by calling out the strengths in the draft. This will reinforce what is working while also creating a tone that allows for suggestions. Even in quite poor examples, there are still a few positives to observe. At a minimum, you might note that they 'had a go' at using the techniques, or that the key ideas are included even if they need significant tightening or reorganising.

▶ Use the language of structure to explain what you want changed. This means, for example, correctly labelling the 'what', the 'why', main message and the top-line structure. If using a deductive chain, then name each element accurately as a statement, comment and recommendation. This helps everyone discuss their structures and get above the detail when working with you and with each other.

▶ Annotate why you have recommended changes. You may use the comments function to do this or add coloured text onto the PowerPoint slide, eg, if:

– ideas are not parallel, you might say, 'I have tweaked the format of these sentences so the ideas belong together. It is then easier to see if the section is complete'

– ideas are not well synthesised, you might say, 'I elevated the synthesis to draw out the message for each point'

– ideas are missing, you might say, 'I added two extra points so we deliver a comprehensive case'

– deductive chains are not well linked, you might say, 'I have more tightly connected the three top-line points so the reader is fully persuaded before they get to the recommendation'.

Now it's time to see how an example evolves so you can see the difference between strong and weak.

▶ Review an example to see the difference between strong and weak

I love helping clients see what is possible. When working with professionals of mixed communication ability, it can be hard to know what good really looks like.

To help with that I will give you the opportunity to review an IT strategy example as we iterate it from 'just OK' to much, much better.

I'll first introduce the situation around that paper before working through each step in the Scan, Score and Share journey with you.

Step 1: Understand the context. The executive needed board approval for their new IT strategy

In this situation an industry body needed to better align their IT strategy with their business strategy.

The IT environment in their organisation was relatively simple and not terribly mature.

The relationship between the executive and the board was cordial and familiar, given the organisation was small and the team was high-performing.

This is good news in reviewing this draft, as we can put stakeholder complexities to the side and focus on the messaging alone.

Step 2: Scan, don't read, the draft

I encourage you to scan the structure on the facing page, keeping in mind the high-level structuring principles I covered in the last chapter. Here's a quick recap:

- Focus first on the big-picture structure. Remember Fido? We are looking to see whether he is structurally sound first, using that as clues to find deeper problems. This means looking at the size of sections and the number of items in each.
- Avoid reading anything more than the occasional word just yet.
- Note down your high-level observations, for the sake of this exercise to reinforce what you are doing here now.
- Remember this should take seconds.

Even if it seems odd, resist the temptation to read deeply just yet. Just scan it, record the ideas as they occur to you, and then review my notes. We will go deep shortly.

Exercise: Scan this draft

Company X wanted to review the IT environment from a business lens and assess fit for purpose.

Cloud and IT strategy existed, but it was not developed in response to the business strategic priorities.

What is the best IT strategy for Company X moving forward to ensure we enable our strategic objectives and delivery?

Answer: Six strategy themes were identified that will deliver and align with IT Strategy. Four viable initiatives were identified for the coming FY with an implementation will cost of $2.4m; however, each is independent in its delivery.

Initiative 1: Foundational enhancements to stakeholder and third-party interactions	Initiative 2: Migrate office productivity & collaboration tools, Tool 1 and Tool 2 from Treasury-hosted environment to Microsoft Cloud	Initiative 3: Digital Records Management	Initiative 4: Secure response and recoverable foundations
Outcome: Enhanced stakeholder and third-party interactions.	**Outcome:** • 20% reduction in annual IT operating costs. • Improved productivity through reduced complexity for users. • Enhanced office collaboration and productivity tools.	**Outcome:** Enhanced stakeholder and third-party interactions.	**Outcome:** Improved information security and business recoverability.
Cost: XXXX	**Cost:** XXXX	**Cost:** XXXX	**Cost:** XXXX
High-level activities: • Foundational single view of customer in CRM. • Redesign website. • Social publishing (LinkedIn).	**High-level activities:** • Migration of existing applications & tools office productivity & collaborations & associated data. • Develop Multisite backup & DR. • Develop third-party support & maintenance. • Promote new ways of working using new collaboration tools.	**High-level activities:** • Define current data and records. • Develop SharePoint libraries to store digitised records. • Scan and upload paper records.	**High-level activities:** • Horizon 1: Half yearly cyber security review & IT security risk reviewed by internal audit. • Horizon 2: Half-yearly DR tests & multisite disaster recovery for business applications.

Step 3: Compare our notes

As with most structures, some things work in this draft, while others don't.

Several aspects of the structure work well

1. The 'what', 'why' and 'question' are about the right length. They are not 'bulging' with background, nor are they just a couple of words.
2. Each of the four supporting points starts with a category, which tells me they are 'the same kind of thing' or, as I call it, conceptually aligned or 'parallel'.
3. A healthy number of supporting points has been included at the top line and also within each section underneath.

Some other aspects require attention

1. The main message box is bulging with too many words.
2. The main message box has two sentences, when it should have only one.
3. The ideas supporting each initiative are chunked by category. I can see this because they are single, bolded words. This shows that the ideas are not fully formed as messages.

So, without even reading the words on the page, we can spot some areas for improvement.

Given the shape has problems, we need to diagnose further to better understand the nature of those problems.

Step 4: SCORE to identify deeper issues

Before reading this section, go back to the deeper SCORE questions and conduct your own review. You may like to flip between that page and the one-pager, or perhaps photocopy the SCORE questions to avoid page flipping. Then come back and compare against my review. Here are my notes.

S – Sets the scene – The introduction and main message do not set the right scene quickly

On the next page I share my notes on the introduction. I revisit the questions I use to assess whether an introduction sets the audience up well as I review the IT strategy example.

As you will see, all the information is there – but the audience has to work too hard to find the message.

This is one of the most common challenges I see and it occurs because the author's thinking wasn't complete.

The IT strategy introduction is off topic, leading to a rambling main message

Scene-setting questions	Comments
Does the draft provide context by explaining WHAT topic is being discussed early? This might be a known problem, opportunity or observation that will be the focus for the paper. Here's the original text: Company X wanted to review the IT environment from a business lens and assess fit for purpose.	It is too general. Doesn't drill into the actual issue at hand: the disconnect between the cloud and IT strategies and the business's strategic priorities.
Does it introduce the topic in a way that is timely?	No. This describes the purpose of the review that was established some time ago. It is not timely.
Does it quickly remind the audience of what they should already know? May reference and/or link to past papers. No longer than 15% of the total document.	No. It quickly reminds the audience about the wrong issue. They do know that they wanted to review the IT environment from a business lens and assess its fit, but it's not the right topic for this paper.
Does it explain WHY this topic is being discussed with this audience now – i.e. what triggered this communication? Here's the original text: A cloud and IT strategy existed, but it was not developed in response to the business strategic priorities.	It doesn't explain why the topic is being discussed now but rather describes the problem being solved. This information better describes what we are communicating about, and so belongs in the 'what' section above the 'why' in the message map. This is a common challenge as people try to articulate why they are really communicating with this audience right now about the topic they have just introduced.
Does it offer one insightful main message? This single, insightful main message should be visible at first glance and unify the whole paper in 25 words or less. Here's the original text: Six strategy themes were identified that will deliver and align with IT Strategy. Four viable initiatives were identified for the coming FY with an implementation cost of $2.4m; however, each is independent in its delivery.	The main message is too long at 35 words and split over two sentences. It also lacks insight.

C – Conveys the right balance of strategic and operational detail – The example is sound regarding strategy and materiality

This element relies on judgment as well as specific structural tests. Each stakeholder group has different preferences, and these are not static. As their situations change, so can their preferences. I'll expand what I look for before sharing what I saw.

What I look for in general

Firstly, does the author position the narrative within the strategy? This might be the organisational strategy or the one for your specific team, or both. In being useful, the communication needs to help the organisation make progress. Aligning to the strategy is a useful and critical test.

Secondly, does the narrative align with the appropriate materiality thresholds? You may want to refer to the formal materiality thresholds outlined in your organisation's governance framework. If your immediate colleagues or manager aren't sure, you can go to others in your organisation for help. Your company secretary will be able to help you with this if you are engaging your board and senior leaders, or perhaps your CEO's assistant can help for the senior leadership team. It may also help to review past papers and comments from participants in analogous meetings.

What I saw in the IT strategy example

While the information in this story isn't yet well formed, it does position itself well within the strategy and align to materiality thresholds.

O – Organises the ideas in a well-structured hierarchy – Both sample grouping and deductive structures lack synthesis, even though they are MECE

I want to be comprehensive here in illustrating the approach, so will work through this structural review in three parts.

I'll begin reviewing the grouping structure I initially shared with you.

I then offer a poor deductive structure to give you an opportunity to review that structural type also. This also highlights that many stories can be shared many ways.

Lastly, I will ask whether the grouping structure is MECE, ie whether the ideas are mutually exclusive and collectively exhaustive. This test is also relevant to deductive structures, but one example review is I think sufficient.

On the next page, I explain why I think the initial grouping structure is weak. Although the points are obviously grouped, the quality of that grouping is not strong.

The grouping structure lacks synthesis

Grouping questions	Comments
Number: Does each group have two to five ideas? Here is the original text for reference: Initiative 1: Foundational enhancements to stakeholder and third-party interactions Initiative 2: Migrate office productivity and collaboration tools, Tool 1 and Tool 2 from Treasury-hosted environment to Microsoft Cloud Initiative 3: Digital Records Management Initiative 4: Secure response and recoverable foundations	Sort of. There are two to five points in each section, both at the top-line level (in the coloured boxes directly under the main message) and in the supporting levels. However, they are not ideas. One of the supporting ideas, under the third point, is a repeat of the idea under the first point though. This is likely a 'copy-paste error' that needs fixing.
Type: Is each idea the same kind of idea as its peers?	These are nearly all the same type, but are not always 'ideas'. Top-line – these are all labeled 'initiatives', which is an encouraging start. The language used to describe each one is not consistent, though, which makes me ask whether each idea really is an 'initiative'. For example, Digital Records Management is a label or a category, not an initiative. Supporting points – these have been 'bucketed' into topics rather than distilled into messages, which means it is 'insight light'. The 'buckets' collect ideas that relate to the topic rather than to the message. Although in this case these points are in the right section of the story, 'dumping' them rather than synthesising them leaves the audience to tie the messaging together, rather than the author doing their job.
Vertical relationships: Does each idea answer the single natural question prompted by the idea above?	No. The ideas are a random assortment of things 'thrown' into 'buckets' rather than tied together to form messages within a cohesive story. This requires the audience to do too much work and leaves the author exposed to the risk that the audience will misunderstand them, or not read the detail as it is too complicated.
Horizontal order: Are the ideas arranged using a logical order – likely sequence or scale?	Mostly, yes. The top line is ordered by scale, with the most important initiative listed first. The lower levels are mostly well ordered also.

Let's now see how it might look if we used a deductive structure. You will see that I have reused the what, why and question, but have offered a weak main message above an equally weak deductive chain.

You may like to review it against my key evaluation questions. At this stage, just look at the top line. By this I mean the three points that sit right below the main message. Ask yourself these questions:

- Does the main message link with the supporting messaging?
- Do the top-line points form a cohesive deductive structure that leads to one powerful recommendation?
- Are the points that support the top-line chain well grouped?

Review the message map below to see what you think and then compare with my notes to the right.

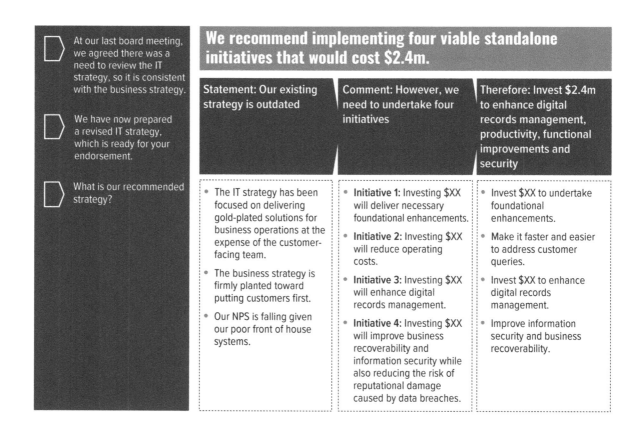

At our last board meeting, we agreed there was a need to review the IT strategy, so it is consistent with the business strategy.

We have now prepared a revised IT strategy, which is ready for your endorsement.

What is our recommended strategy?

We recommend implementing four viable standalone initiatives that would cost $2.4m.

Statement: Our existing strategy is outdated	Comment: However, we need to undertake four initiatives	Therefore: Invest $2.4m to enhance digital records management, productivity, functional improvements and security
• The IT strategy has been focused on delivering gold-plated solutions for business operations at the expense of the customer-facing team. • The business strategy is firmly planted toward putting customers first. • Our NPS is falling given our poor front of house systems.	• **Initiative 1:** Investing $XX will deliver necessary foundational enhancements. • **Initiative 2:** Investing $XX will reduce operating costs. • **Initiative 3:** Investing $XX will enhance digital records management. • **Initiative 4:** Investing $XX will improve business recoverability and information security while also reducing the risk of reputational damage caused by data breaches.	• Invest $XX to undertake foundational enhancements. • Make it faster and easier to address customer queries. • Invest $XX to enhance digital records management. • Improve information security and business recoverability.

This deductive version also lacked synthesis

Questions for the top line	Comments
Does the statement anchor the narrative around one substantive idea that is both new to the audience and broader in scope than the comment? Here is the original text for reference: Our existing strategy is outdated	The statement is broad but so generic that it is hard to evaluate. It is not insightful and is unlikely to be news to decision-makers.
Does the comment focus on one key concept that was introduced in the statement? However, we need to undertake four initiatives	Does not link to the statement. This is a separate idea that is related but not intrinsically linked to the same topic. It is also intellectually blank. All it says is that there are four initiatives; it lacks substance and insight.
Is it reasonable to expect that the audience is persuaded in your recommendation by the time they have read the statement and comment, or does it come as a surprise? Therefore, invest $2.4m to enhance digital records management, productivity, functional improvements and security	No. This appears out of nowhere! The audience is not prepared for the idea that they should invest $2.4 million by reading the top line only. It is also a list of ideas that belongs in the level below rather than a single and insightful point that glues those supporting ideas together.

Questions for the second line	Comments
Are both the statement and comment supported by tightly grouped reasons?	No. The statement is supported by a mix of reasons and statements of fact. For example, 'the business strategy is firmly planted toward putting customers first' is an observation that does not do anything other than describe the existing situation. It is also unlikely to be news. The supporting points under the comment do *try* to explain why spending a certain amount of money will deliver a benefit, but they are weakly expressed. They lack substance.
Is the 'therefore' recommendation supported by tightly grouped actions?	These points are actions, but they are too general to be useful. They do not demonstrate that the author has thought about the actions that need to be undertaken to improve the IT strategy. They are also in mixed format, with the ideas not being parallel. Some include a financial element, but others do not, leaving me wondering if they are free!

Although poorly expressed, the ideas in the grouping are MECE

Although I think the expression in the original grouping message map is poor, the ideas are MECE. They are well categorised and labelled, separate and complete.

Now that you have a view about the integrity of the structure, you need to ask yourself whether it is fit for purpose. It needs to both 'tell the answer' and 'tell the story'.

By this I mean it goes further than explaining what is technically accurate to explaining how this 'answer' can help drive progress.

R – Readies the audience for a productive discussion – I give the grouping half marks

This again requires judgement combined with a good understanding of your stakeholders and their needs.

When I think about readying the audience for a productive discussion, I want them to not only read the communication quickly and easily, but understand it without wasting time. This means they won't take up time in the meeting clarifying the ideas in the paper and potentially delaying or not taking the action you need.

This doesn't assume automatic approval, but that stakeholders will be able to quickly evaluate and discuss it intelligently. See my responses below.

Readiness questions	Comments
Does the message map focus only on matters relevant to the desired outcome?	Yes.
Are the ideas synthesised and summarised at every level into fully formed sentences that *the audience will find insightful?*	No. Many of the points were not ideas, which by definition means they are not fully formed sentences and cannot be insightful.
Are the ideas expressed clearly with little need for clarification?	No. The 'voice over' in the subsequent meeting was needed to cover up for the weaknesses in the individual points and to string them together. The messaging did not stand alone.

E – Engages the audience –This message map only weakly engages the audience

Some organisations use templates to tightly prescribe the way information is presented to senior leaders, while others offer a great degree of freedom.

The key is to understand the requirements of your specific senior stakeholder group and to accommodate those. If unsure, err on the side of formality and respect while avoiding being boring and stiff.

The table below outlines key things to look for, again commenting on the IT strategy grouping. These are again relatively straightforward ideas that require little introduction.

At the one-page stage, ask yourself whether the way your or your team's points are drafted will translate well into the final paper or presentation form.

I do note also that I am providing comments here on a one-pager, rather than a full document. These engagement questions are better suited to the final paper or presentation. I do hope, however, that this quick illustration makes the point.

To drive that home, on the next page I rework both the grouping and deductive versions of the the IT strategy story to show you how much stronger they could have been.

Engagement questions	Comments
Is the messaging easy to skim, regardless of the chosen medium?	The messages were buried inside 'topics' or 'buckets'.
	This makes them hard to find, slowing down the audience and requiring them to do a lot of the thinking work themselves.
Have images, charts and diagrams been used wherever possible to help the audience quickly grasp the ideas?	This is only relevant when reviewing a paper or presentation.
	I will, however, call out one important point. I see clients reworking the message map to remove the main message and sometimes also the top line points. Changing this visual format does not help the author synthesise their points, nor the audience grasp them.

This stronger grouping structure suits an audience that needs little persuasion

At our last board meeting, we agreed there was a need to review the IT strategy, so it is consistent with the business strategy.

We have now prepared a revised IT strategy, which is ready for your endorsement.

What is your recommended strategy?

We recommend implementing four viable standalone initiatives that would cost $2.4m to implement during 2023 to realign our IT and business strategies.

Initiative 1: Invest $XX to undertake foundational enhancements to stakeholder and third-party interactions.	**Initiative 2:** Invest $XX to reduce operating costs through improved productivity and collaboration tools.	**Initiative 3:** Invest $XX to enhance Digital Records Management.	**Initiative 3:** Invest $XX to improve information security and business recoverability.
• Create foundational single view of customers in the CRM. • Redesign website. • Improve social publishing (LinkedIn).	• Migrate existing applications and office productivity and collaboration tools and associated data from xxx to Microsoft Cloud. • Develop multi-site backup and DR. • Develop third-party support and maintenance agreements. • Promote new ways of working using new collaboration tools.	• Define current data and records. • Develop SharePoint libraries to store digitised records. • Scan and upload paper records.	• **Horizon 1:** Undertake half yearly cyber security review and IT security risk audit, which will be reviewed by internal audit. • **Horizon 2:** Undertake half yearly DR tests and multi-site disaster recovery for business applications.

This stronger deductive version is for an audience that needs more persuasion than the grouping offers

At our last board meeting, we agreed there was a need to review the IT strategy, so it is consistent with the business strategy.

We have now prepared a revised IT strategy, which is ready for your endorsement.

What is our recommended strategy?

We recommend implementing four viable standalone initiatives that would cost $2.4m to implement during 2023 to realign our IT and business strategies.

Our existing IT strategy is out of line with our business strategy, hampering our ability to capture and serve customers.

However, implementing four key initiatives at a cost of $2.4m will realign our IT and business strategies.

Therefore, we recommend investing $2.4m to implement four key initiatives.

- The IT strategy has been focused on delivering gold-plated solutions for business operations at the expense of the customer-facing team.
- The business strategy is firmly focused on growing our customer base by delivering outstanding products and services.
- Our NPS is falling given our poor front of house systems.

- **Initiative 1:** Investing $XX will deliver necessary foundational enhancements to improve stakeholder and customer experience.
- **Initiative 2:** Investing $XX will reduce operating costs through improved productivity and collaboration tools.
- **Initiative 3:** Investing $XX will enhance digital records management, making it faster and easier to answer customer queries.
- **Initiative 4:** Investing $XX will improve business recoverability and information security while also reducing the risk of reputational damage caused by data breaches.

- **Initiative 1:** Invest $XX to undertake foundational enhancements.
- **Initiative 2:** Invest $XX to improve productivity and collaboration tools.
- **Initiative 3:** Invest $XX to enhance digital records management.
- **Initiative 4:** Invest $XX to improve information security and business recoverability.

CHAPTER 6

Finalise your document so it engages decision-makers

Now your thinking is clear and the team has finalised their one-pager, they will translate it into a document. Your next step is to review the document to gain confidence that it matches your needs and expectations. Ideally, this will involve a quick Scan, Score, Share process where you again lean on the structure of the messaging to evaluate the quality of the material.

I recommend tightly linking the hierarchy of your messaging with the formatting of your document – whether it is an email, a paper or a presentation. To do this, you need to do five things:

▶ Understand the connection between message maps and documents.

▶ Connect the dots using the 105 reports example.

▶ Factor in corporate templates where needed.

▶ Know how to quickly review papers and presentations.

▶ Present with polish.

▶ Understand the connection between message maps and documents

Having invested in preparing a tightly structured and insightful message map, now is not the time for your team to bury the insights.

To that end, I recommend maintaining a strong connection between your message map and your document. This ensures ideas are easy to find. Here are the three steps to take:

1. Tailor the title to convey the right tone.
2. Begin with a well-structured executive summary.
3. Visualise the messaging so the audience can easily skim the headlines.

Tailor the title to convey the right tone

I differentiate my approach for the title to suit the sensitivity of the messaging.

When a message is sensitive or perhaps unusually controversial, it pays to hold it back until you can introduce it properly. In these instances, I recommend using the title to describe what you are discussing. Said another way, I use the type of meeting as the title. For example, for the 105 reports example you might say 'Legacy Reports Project Update'.

If the main message is not so sensitive or is just plain good news, then tighten it to become akin to a newspaper headline. For example, you might say 'Legacy Reports Project on track across all key areas'. This approach would be risky for this example, which involves a delicate message. Beginning with a title that says something like, 'Need to decide whether to spend

more or renegotiate with the regulator for Report Project' would also be provocative. In situations like these, you might choose a different path.

You might want to draw stakeholder attention to the importance of the current juncture without giving the game away. You might say something like, 'Critical decision point for Legacy Reports Project'. You could even nudge the urgency further by saying something like, 'Critical decision needed to determine direction for Legacy Reports Project'.

Your title choice is determined by your judgement as to what will be most effective in your current situation.

Once that is established, you can move to the executive summary.

I have outlined options for easy reference below.

Type	Options for titles
Meeting type	Legacy Reports Project Update
Main message	Need to decide whether to spend more or negotiate with regulator
Discussion topic	Critical decision point for Legacy Reports Project
The ask	Critical decision needed to determine direction for Legacy Reports Project

Begin with a well-structured executive summary

If your document is longer than half a page, you need an executive summary. Regardless of the format, this will include your introduction, main message and top-line points.

Here a few thoughts to help you prepare yours.

1. Adjust the order of the items in the introduction to suit your tone. Using the 'classic order' I introduced earlier ('What', 'Why' and then main message) is clear and straightforward, but slightly softer than some other options. In contrast, beginning with the main message or 'why' strengthens the tone. If you experiment with this for an example of your own, you will see what I mean. Emails are the perfect playground as you will quickly see the tonal shifts.

2. Next, offer the top-line points as a list, or even better, use a diagram to visualise the concepts you are discussing. The easiest way to find a suitable framework or diagram is to use an image library. Many organisations have them, and my colleague Neil Young offers such a library with 300 high-quality visuals inside. You can download a sample inside the Clarity Hub, or purchase the whole 300 on my site[11].

3. Expand the executive summary if needed. If you and your team are preparing a lengthy paper, you may include a short paragraph for each point in the executive summary. Most business communication, however, only needs the top-line points.

Visualise the messaging so the audience can easily skim the headlines

I encourage you to use visual cues to differentiate the value of each point. The bigger the idea, the more visible it should be so the audience can grasp it immediately.

If you skim this book, you will see this technique in play. If your formatting matches the hierarchy of your messaging, your audience will be able to quickly find what they need. This is especially important for business communication. Your audience is not sitting on a beach relaxing into a novel. They are working against the clock to add value. Your communication needs to help them do that.

---

11   ClarityFirstProgram.com/ImageLibrary

▶ Connect the dots using the 105 reports example

The coming pages showcase how the 105 reports message map operates in both presentation and paper format. Translating the message map structure into document format is relatively straightforward, so I will illustrate more than explain using an annotated example.

Before I go there, however, I will call out some practicalities for each format.

Practicalities for presentations

I have kept this presentation fairly high level on the assumption that the steering committee was familiar with the issues and could refer to detailed financial breakdowns in the appendix.

This makes it easy to see the links between the message map and the document.

Should you want some more complex examples, check out my PowerPoint Toolkit, which illustrates how some very different structures play out in PowerPoint. At the time of writing I offer seven sanitised real-world professional examples, but plan to add more.[12]

Practicalities for papers

The 105 reports example needs to be presented to a senior decision-making body which uses a template. Here are my thoughts about how I link simple templates with a message map:

▶ The 'Recommendation' section usually includes the main message, explaining what you are asking the decision-making group to sign off against. In this case, the recommendation is more general so I handled it differently.

▶ The 'Executive summary' provides a complete high-level overview of the story, structured to match the message map itself.

▶ The 'Discussion' unpacks each of the supporting points from the high-level story, offering more detail on each.

▶ The 'Attachments' section caters for the extra detail a manager might require to be confident in the substance. Members of this leadership group may also want to review the financials, but some will trust the managers to have reviewed these thoroughly, rendering the attachments section the most appropriate place for these details.

---

12 ClarityFirstProgram.com/ImageLibrary

This 105 Reports message map sets up the storyboard, the PowerPoint deck and the Board Paper

Meeting regulatory requirements requires us to transition all 105 legacy reports into the case system by the end of this financial year. We have now reviewed the associated work plans and received updated estimates.

We are now ready to share those estimates with you along with potential ways forward.

What are you suggesting?

Delivering the 105 reports means either investing $1.2m to $2m more over the coming two years or renegotiating requirements with the regulator.

Despite stress testing all budgets, we can't transition all 105 regulatory reports within the agreed $2m budget this financial year.	This means we need to make trade-offs when finalising the project workplans.	Therefore, we ask you to advise which tradeoffs we can make.
Updated estimates for database came back at $2m, which is 2.5 x the original budget due to more comprehensive scoping. **Budgets for other aspects of the work have not materially changed.** • Workflow remains same. • API linking ditto. • Operational teams ditto. **Work required for reports identified since June last year has not been factored in.**	**We could meet the scope by spending $1.2m to $2m more over the coming two years.** • We could deliver everything in FY23 with $1.2m more during FY23, or • We could deliver some in FY23, some in FY24 with $2m or more in total. **We could renegotiate scope or time with the regulator.** • We could limit the scope and deliver only the top 70 reports by FY23 (fix existing 36, do another 35ish) within the current budget, or • We could seek agreement from the regulator to further extend the project and deliver all at a later date.	**Decide whether to spend more ...** • Decide whether to increase funding by $1.2m for FY23. • Decide whether to budget $2m more for the project in total and roll into next year. **Decide whether to renegotiate ...** • Decide whether to pitch the regulator to accept the top 70 reports as adequate for FY23. • Decide whether to seek extensions.

Title page explains why we are presenting re: the legacy reports

BIG BANK

LEGACY REPORT PROGRAM – CRITICAL DECISION POINT RE: PATH FORWARD FOR 105 REPORTS

PROGRAM STEERCO
JULY, 2023

Background page offers the what and why (hide when presenting)

Meeting regulatory requirements requires us to transition all 105 legacy reports into the case system by the end of this financial year.

We have now reviewed plans and estimates and are ready to discuss potential ways forward.

Executive summary offers high level message + navigation aid

We need to decide to either spend $1.2 million to $2 million more over the coming two years or to renegotiate requirements with the regulator

01 Despite stress-testing all budgets, we can't transition all 105 regulatory reports within the agreed $2 million budget this financial year.

02 This means we need to decide which tradeoffs to make as we rescope the project.

03 Therefore, we ask you to advise which tradeoffs we can make in rescoping the project.

Navigator in top right corner of each page

Despite stress-testing all budgets, we can't transition all 105 regulatory reports within the agreed $2 million budget this financial year

01 Updated estimates for database came back at $2m, which is 2.5 x the original budget due to more comprehensive scoping. (See appendix for breakdown.)

02 Budgets for other aspects of the work have not materially changed. Costs for workflow, API linking, and operational aspects remain steady.

03 Work required for reports identified since June last year has not been factored in.

Title of each page is the message

This means we need to make trade-offs when rescoping the project workplans

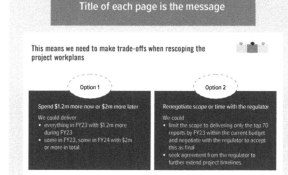

Option 1

Spend $1.2m more now or $2m more later

We could deliver
- everything in FY23 with $1.2m more during FY23
- some in FY23, some in FY24 with $2m or more in total.

Option 2

Renegotiate scope or time with the regulator

We could
- limit the scope to delivering only the top 70 reports by FY23 within the current budget and negotiate with the regulator to accept this as final
- seek agreement from the regulator to further extend project timelines.

Repetitive wording removed and language tightened

We ask you to advise which trade-offs we can make

We need to decide whether we

Spend more by
1. increasing funding by $1.2m for FY23
2. budgeting $2m more for the project in total and roll into next year.

Renegotiate by
1. accepting the top 70 reports in FY23 as adequate and convincing the regulator to agree
2. seeking extensions from the regulator.

Meeting regulatory requirements requires us to transition all 105 legacy reports into the case system by the end of this financial year.

We have now reviewed plans and estimates and are ready to discuss potential ways forward.

We need to decide
to either spend
$1.2 million to
$2 million more over
the coming two
years or to
renegotiate
requirements with
the regulator

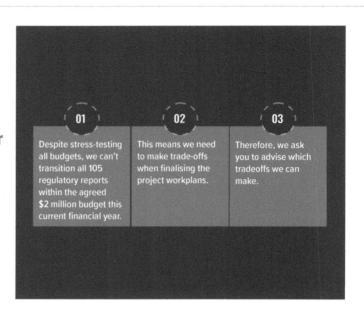

Despite stress-testing all budgets, we can't transition all 105 regulatory
reports within the agreed $2 million budget this financial year

01 Updated estimates for database came back at $2m, which is 2.5 x the original budget due to a more comprehensive scoping. (See appendix for breakdown.)

02 Budgets for other aspects of the work have not materially changed. Costs for workflow, API linking, and operational aspects remain steady.

03 Work required for reports identified since June last year has not been factored in.

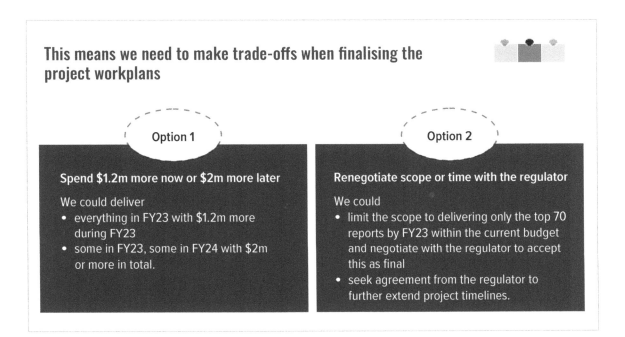

This means we need to make trade-offs when finalising the project workplans

Option 1

Spend $1.2m more now or $2m more later

We could deliver
- everything in FY23 with $1.2m more during FY23
- some in FY23, some in FY24 with $2m or more in total.

Option 2

Renegotiate scope or time with the regulator

We could
- limit the scope to delivering only the top 70 reports by FY23 within the current budget and negotiate with the regulator to accept this as final
- seek agreement from the regulator to further extend project timelines.

We ask you to advise which trade-offs we can make

We need to decide whether we

Spend more by
1. increasing funding by $1.2m for FY23
2. budgeting $2m more for the project in total and roll into next year.

Renegotiate by
1. accepting the top 70 reports in FY23 as adequate and convincing the regulator to agree
2. seeking extensions from the regulator.

The Regulatory Projects Steering Committee advises which trade-offs the team can make to finalise workplans for 2024.

EXECUTIVE SUMMARY

Meeting regulatory requirements requires us to transition all 105 legacy reports into the case system by the end of this financial year. We have now reviewed the plans and estimates and are ready to discuss potential ways forward.

In sum, we need to decide to either spend an extra $1.2 million to $2 million over the coming two years or renegotiate requirements with the regulator. Here is an outline of our high-level position before going into more detail below.

1. Despite stress testing all budgets, we can't transition all 105 regulatory reports within the agreed $2 million budget this financial year.
2. This means we need to make trade-offs when finalising the workplans.
3. As a result, we ask you to advise which trade-offs we can make.

DISCUSSION

Despite stress testing all budgets, we can't transition all 105 regulatory reports within the agreed $2 million budget this financial year. After conducting the thorough review that you requested, we found

- Updated estimates for database came back at $2 million – 2.5 times the original budget due to a more comprehensive scoping. (See appendix for breakdown.)
- Budgets for other aspects of the work have not materially changed. Costs for workflow, API linking, and operational aspects remain steady.
- Any reports that have been identified as needing to be reworked since June last year have not been factored into this.

This means we need to make trade-offs when finalising the workplans. Given these trade-offs require your endorsement to be implemented, we offer alternatives for your consideration.

Option 1: Spend $1.2 million more now or $2 million more later. We could then deliver either

- everything in FY23 with $1.2 million more during FY23
- some in FY23, some in FY24 with $2 million or more.

Option 2: Renegotiate scope or time with the regulator. If taking this path, we could

- limit the scope to delivering only the top 70 reports by FY23 within the current budget and negotiate with the regulator to accept this as final, or
- seek agreement from the regulator to further extend project timelines.

As a result, we ask you to advise which trade-offs we can make. This involves deciding whether to

- Spend more by either
  - increasing funding by $1.2 million for FY23, or
  - budgeting $2 million more for the project in total and roll into next year.
- Renegotiate by either
  - accepting the top 70 reports in FY23 as adequate and convincing the regulator to agree, or
  - seeking extensions from the regulator.

We understand this is not the outcome you were hoping for but look forward to your decision as to the best way forward.

ATTACHMENTS

Detailed financial breakdown of the updated financial estimates for all aspects of the 105 reports project.

SUBMITTED BY

Ryan Bloggs, Program Manager, Regulatory Projects

▶ Factor in corporate templates where needed

Templates for business cases, updates and other reports are used widely to ensure an author has 'thought about everything'. They are often also quite detailed, telling you what topic to cover where.

They rarely form a basis for a strong narrative. Assuming that all you need to do is fill in the sections can impede your ability to engage decision-makers.

If you are fortunate, your template will allow room for an executive summary. This is 'the money spot' where you add your narrative – either just the top line structure for the story or the extra layer you will have mapped out with your team on your one pager. However, it is not always that easy.

In this section, I offer suggestions to help use message mapping alongside the key kinds of corporate templates I see in play.

This involves 'wrangling' a template to accommodate message maps in four ways:

1. *Use your message map as your executive summary.* Many templates for business cases or updates include a box for your executive summary. Some people add the message map as an image, but most insert the content in text form.

2. *Use your message map as speaking notes.* Reports may be fixed in structure, sometimes because they are automatically generated. When this happens, you may want to summarise the information in the report into a message map that you use to introduce the presentation.

You may go a step further and explain the implications of the report findings, if that is helpful.

Either way, you could include the narrative in the email that you attach the report to or deliver it verbally (ideally) before or (if necessary) after you dive into the data.

3. *Create separate mini stories for each section.* Where you have a series of topics you must cover, I suggest working out what the message for each of these points is. Add that message after the section title. Here is an example where two topics are in play for a retailer's routine leadership update:

> Sales – 12% growth driven by increased foot traffic from shopping centre campaign.

> Safety – Slips and trips stable at X for June with no major incidents.

These page titles can then form the substance of your executive summary. Once you line them up on a page you can stand back and ask yourself what overall message they suggest, and use that as your main message for the deck.

4. *Add an executive summary page up front.* Where this is not typically included, I suggest adding a full narrative ('What', 'Why', main message and supporting points) at the front. If in PowerPoint, this would be the first page after the title page; if in prose, then as close to the front of the document as you can get it.

Now you are comfortable with the links between a message map and a paper or presentation, let's look at how to review your own draft.

▶ Know how to quickly review papers and presentations

Given the tight link between the message map and the document, we can revert to a tailored version of the Scan, Score, Share technique to quickly review a draft.

Here is how I do that, whether working freeform or within a corporate template.

SCAN the high-level messaging to see if it matches the one-pager

As with the one-pager, my initial scan takes seconds.

The first thing I check is whether the document telegraphs the messaging so it is easy to find. Then I scan the structure of the messaging. I offer here the key things I look for in each case.

First: Is the messaging easy to find?

Even though I don't have the structure of the message map to guide me here, I can easily check the messaging structure other ways.

Here are the initial questions I ask myself in conducting this quick scan:

1. Is there a short executive summary at the start that matches the message map?
2. Can I see the main message without looking hard for it?
3. Do the top-line messages stand out in larger font with more white space around them than lower-level points?
4. Can I skim the hierarchy of the messaging without reading the details?

Then I ask: Is the structure strong?

Here I am looking for very similar things as I do when reviewing a one-pager, eg,

1. Are there two to five sections at every level?
2. If there are three points at any level, do they look grouped or deductive?
   a. If grouped, do the words follow a common language pattern?
   b. If deductive, is it obvious that the statement leads to the comment and then the recommendation?
3. Are the proportions right? (That is, are there any sections that seem really big while others are tiny, hinting at problems with synthesis?)

Once I have undertaken this quick scan I decide what is next. If it looks terrific, that's easy: I'm done. If I saw problems, I need to repair them.

SCORE the document to draw out areas for improvement

If I decide to analyse further, I try to work out whether the problems are to do with the visualisation of the message, or whether the message has come undone.

If the problems relate to visualisation, where the message is intact but poorly represented, I better align it with the message map. If I fear the message itself has come undone, I revert back to the message map to find the disconnect.

This may involve backfilling information into the one-pager and reviewing it against the SCORE framework to check the message has maintained its integrity.

This disconnect between message and document typically occurs when the author has raced off to prepare the paper or presentation without thoroughly locking down the message with their peers and their manager.

The challenge with refining the thinking inside the document is that the high-level messaging gets lost. This then makes the document harder to follow, requiring late changes from you.

Although late changes are hard to eradicate, focusing the thinking work around the message map will minimise them.

SHARE your observations to help settle the document

There are many ways to share your observations with your colleagues, which will be driven by practicalities all round. Here are some thoughts to help.

Choose the best mode

Your colleagues' availability and capability will help you decide how to approach this conversation. Do you:

1. Rework it yourself to better align the new messaging with the document format? This may be necessary if they don't use this technique for thinking through their messaging.
2. Meet to ask them to talk through the shift in messaging so you can fine-tune the document together?
3. Help them diagnose the thinking problems within the document by walking through the SCORE framework together?

Ultimately you and your manager will balance the amount of time everyone has before the document must be submitted with the amount of improvement needed when deciding how to proceed.

Mix clarity with tact

Regardless of your chosen path, I offer three suggestions for sharing your observations:

1. *Use message mapping language to help your team embed the concepts in their minds.* If the problem is with the main message – say so. If the 'what' is bulging, offering too much background – say so. If the ideas are not well grouped or not tightly deductive – say so.
2. *Focus on the structure and substance of the message more than the language style.* Even though we always want communication for senior audiences to *look* good, it is more important to *be* good.
   Even if your colleague uses a different speaking voice or illustrates things in a way that you would not, the document may still be fit for purpose.
   Everyone knows these documents are a team effort. It is fair to ask yourself how much of your weekend you and your colleagues should spend making something that is substantively on point 'look and feel' like the same person wrote it.
   I even know some companies that punish people for over investing in making presentations look and feel beautiful. They are ruthless about focusing on where the value lies.

3. *Tread lightly where the problems are substantial.* Here are three thoughts to help with that:

   a. *Use questions to diagnose what is going on.* Unless I have explicit permission from my clients to be blunt (some prefer that!), I avoid describing the problems myself. Rather, I ask questions about the structure that lead them to see the problems themselves.

   b. *Offer suggestions rather than critique.* Where someone isn't getting where I want them to go through my questioning techniques, I turn to 'what if we ...' to highlight other ways of handling the draft.

   c. *Ask them to walk through the narrative verbally.* If I see big problems, I might ask them to tell me about the structure. I often find they can tell the story better than they can write it, and this saves much time.

      This can be faster than working through the document line by line, which can be torturous and slow when the writing (and thinking!) is muddled.

Experience tells me less rework on the document will be required than in the past, which will release you to think more about how you actually present to your audience.

▶ Present with polish

Whatever the end deliverable looks like, you likely need to have early-stage discussions about the messaging, present it formally, or both.

At this stage you want your delivery to help rather than hinder your progress.

Framing and flagging help your audience keep up with you, while flexing to their responses allows for maximum engagement. Here are ideas to help with all three.

Frame where you are going so your audience knows what to expect

Framing enables you to get above the narrative itself to explain where you are going with the discussion. It provides both you and the audience with confidence by helping you set expectations and direct the discussion.

Framing also helps your decision-makers tune in to your topic from the beginning.

Ideally, you will begin with a short recap of the paper to remind your audience what you are there to discuss. You might say something like this:

> Today I will recap on our recommendation for supporting the next phase of Project X before opening for discussion. I'll quickly set the scene and then be up-front about our recommendation before giving you our high-level thinking. Then we can work through the details together.

As an example, a senior government client of mine uses the following wonderful frame when he has to share difficult news:

> Today we are here to talk about X difficult topic. Before I start, I want you to know that I have some bad news and some good news, but it will be all right in the end.

This is particularly useful when you have used the Oh Dear pattern, which opens by introducing a problem that is new to your audience.

Carefully done, this can engage your audience in a new problem and prepare them to hear your recommended solution.

Care is paramount with Oh Dear, and framing helps with that.

Flag where you are up to so your audience can keep up

Let your audience know each time you transition from one section of the structure to the next.

Your flag can be as simple as saying, 'Now to my third point: risks'. Or, perhaps something like, 'Now that we have covered off on how this recommendation aligns with our overall strategy, I'll share our thoughts on the returns'.

I keep flags general, describing what I am talking about rather than what I am saying.

Flex to your audience's responses for maximum engagement

Although confidence in your ability to present your paper or PowerPoint is important, you may not need to present as much as you think. Ideally, your decision-makers will already have read your paper. They usually prefer to have a discussion than just listen and may be short on time.

Many a group has found that their audience doesn't want to discuss their topic in the same way they do. You might be ready to make a recommendation for a new approach, while they might want to talk to you in depth about changes in the industry, or perhaps revisit key issues from the previous meeting.

In these instances, you have little choice but to address their issues first. Once these are settled, you will have an appreciative audience, but be short on time.

Equally, many a group has been allocated 30 minutes in a senior meeting only to be squeezed to just five as previous presentations have run over time. The worst thing to do at this point is to assume you need to speak fast to 'cover everything'.

Let me share an example here to illustrate how to handle this common challenge.

After a whole-day board meeting, Mary's exec team came together at 6 pm, which was an hour later than planned, for a one-hour meeting to discuss three issues.

Mary drew the short straw: she was third out of the three and now looking to present to an exhausted leadership at about 6.50 pm.

As the meeting progressed, each of her peers began with something like this:

> 'I realise it's been a long day, so I'll keep it short'.

They then did the opposite, taking the leaders on a convoluted journey through every detail of their presentation and working toward the big reveal at the end.

If the leaders were tired at the start of the meeting, their minds were now 'mush'.

Mary's solution was to share the high-level messaging using the executive summary as her guide.

Within five minutes she had her approval and a grateful exec team in her corner after three questions.

Her comment afterwards was that the thinking she and her team did to prepare the message map was the key. Being clear about the story in her own mind enabled her to cover on the high-level ideas quickly, insightfully and calmly.

This is a story I have heard time and again, even though some clients worry they are spending too much time thinking up-front.

Now you can see how to use the message map when preparing your communication, it is time to embed the learning from this new process into the team's ways of working.

In the next chapter, I offer thoughts on how you can hardwire feedback into your regular rhythm so you can improve, presentation by presentation.

CHAPTER 7

Feed back and feed forward to capture learnings

A significant missed opportunity arises when you, your colleagues and your manager don't take a few moments to reflect on what went well, what didn't and what you and the team can do differently next time.

This step is often ignored as everyone moves quickly forward from one task to the next. It can be hard to remember to take five minutes to capitalise on what everyone learned from a paper or presentation.

It can also be consciously avoided for fear of receiving criticism that feels personal rather than ideas for improvement. Communication can feel like it is a more personal aspect of work than more technical areas, which can magnify this fear.

In this short chapter I offer some thoughts on how to get the most out of your communication experience, so you and your colleagues can flourish together.

I suggest finding opportunities to:

- Assess the quality of conversation that your paper or presentation stimulated.
- Better understand individual stakeholders.
- Capture reactions to the presentation itself.
- Optimise collaboration.

The following sections include some questions to stimulate your thinking in each of these four areas.

▶ Assess the quality of the conversation that your paper or presentation stimulated

It should come as no surprise to say that not all conversations are equally valuable. Even if you were in the meeting where your paper was presented, you may pick up on different things than your colleagues and your manager, so it's worth unpacking this a bit.

Here are some questions to help flush out that conversation:

- ▶ What proportion of the discussion was spent clarifying the ideas in the paper rather than discussing its substance?

- ▶ Was the discussion only with the subject matter experts who contributed, or did others also get involved?

- ▶ Was the conversation polarised toward one or two vocal people, or did everyone participate?

- ▶ Did you (and your manager) get a valuable answer from the group, even if it wasn't the one you wanted?

If the conversation was deeply focused on the material issues and involved many people on the decision-making group, you can be confident the paper did its job. This doesn't mean it couldn't have been better, but it is a good sign regardless.

▶ Better understand individual stakeholders

Every time you engage with someone or a group you learn more about their preferences. It may help to consolidate your observations from this one presentation to feed into future paper preparation. Here are a couple of questions to stimulate that discussion:

- ▶ What did you (or your manager) learn about stakeholders' positions and strategies in relation to this topic?

- ▶ Did any stakeholders have a strong view one way or another about the issue?

- ▶ Did any stakeholders seem less interested than you expected?

Individuals and groups change over time so even if you and your manager think you have a good understanding of the group, be alert to shifts.

▶ Capture reactions to the presentation itself

Even if you want to hold back on asking for communication feedback, I am going to suggest you do it anyway. Here are a couple of thought starters:

▶ Did anyone comment about the quality of the paper (or not)? No news is often good news, but not always.

▶ What worked well regarding the substance and the structure of the paper or presentation?

▶ Did you miss any key messages?

▶ Did the framing work?

▶ What do stakeholders suggest you do differently next time?

▶ Optimise collaboration

The quality of the outcome may be aligned with the quality of the process. Take a few moments to reflect on how the process itself went for you, and perhaps for your team as a whole:

▶ Did you provide the message maps and the documents to the relevant leader with sufficient time for them to review them?

▶ Did you and the team pay sufficient attention to the quality of the thinking before sending it up the chain for review?

▶ Did you peer-review the message map and separately, the document, with colleagues before sending to your manager for review?

I hope these questions and thought starters are useful, and I look forward now to helping you elevate your skills as a whole.

PART III

STAY THE COURSE

CHAPTER 8

Flourish into the long term

A common idea in learning and development is that 10 per cent of the benefit comes from coursework and training, 20 per cent comes from coaching and 70 per cent comes from challenging assignments that have direct relevance to someone's role[13].

This means that much of the real learning happens over time and on the job. This is why practice is so important.

This sums up why I have written this book. I can only help you so far, however; most of the work is up to you in the near and longer term. To help you keep on track I offer a series of supporting tools available in your free month's access of the Clarity Hub[14].

So, having helped you build your skills and adjust your operating rhythm, in this chapter I offer ideas to help you flourish into the longer term.

I have broken the timeline into two sections:

1. the first three months to fine-tune skills and behaviours
2. thereafter for making the new ways of working 'stick'.

▶ First three months: Fine-tune skills and behaviours

Now that you are familiar with message maps, it's time to fine-tune skills and behaviours.

You want to go beyond 'knowing a few good ideas' to being really good at mapping messages. To help, I offer messages to bring your colleagues along with you, materials to remove barriers and prompt behaviours, measurement to identify wins and areas for further focus, and motivation to keep moving forward as novelty wanes. I unpack each of these here.

---

13 Michael Lombardo and Robert Eichinger expressed the rationale behind this 70:20:10 model in *The Career Architect Development Planner*.
14 ClarityFirstProgram.com/ClarityHub

Messages to help bring your colleagues along with you

If you have taken on implementing the ideas in this book on your own, you may want to share your journey with your manager and your colleagues.

In most cases, I have found those receiving communication crafted using message maps have been highly receptive. However, it helps to stay on the front foot. Here are three ideas to help:

1. Explain to your manager that you are exploring some new communication techniques that you hope will lift the clarity and quality of your messaging. Convey three things alongside a request for patience as you experiment to master it:

    –   The technique helps you structure your messaging for all key communication around one single idea.

    –   This idea will be introduced early in the communication, regardless of whether you are writing an email, a paper or a presentation.

    –   The technique is based on work done at McKinsey by Barbara Minto and her team, and then further refined by other ex-McKinsey communication specialists.

(They may have heard of the Minto Pyramid Principle® or structured thinking, particularly if they have worked in consulting environments.)

2. Offer to share insights you have learned from the book with a colleague, or perhaps your whole team.

    Your manager may appreciate you taking the effort to build the team's skills, and forcing yourself to share the ideas will deepen your own understanding.

3. Draft a script to help you explain what you are doing to those not familiar with mapping messages before sharing a draft with them. Here is an example that may help. (You can also find this example in the appendix and saved as a Word doc in the Clarity Hub to save you retyping.)

Hi colleague/boss,

I have been thinking about *X* issue and have outlined my early thinking on a page for your consideration.

Before you review it, I'd like to explain how the page works so the diagram makes sense to you.

1. It is a discussion draft. Although the ideas are, I hope, in a clear and logical place within the structure,

the ideas are very much open for debate.

2. The draft outlines my current thinking in a way that may seem more direct than usual. You will see that the ideas are anchored around a single message that is crafted as a point of view.

   The technique I am using flushes out the main thought up-front, before diving into the details.

3. Once we agree on the messaging, we can turn these ideas into a well-structured document. I would like to hold off on preparing the document until we agree on the ideas to minimise rework.

   Focusing on the one-pager first will keep us focused on the main ideas and encourage us to 'nail these' without being distracted by document formatting. My experience so far suggests we can save time this way.

I look forward to discussing issue *X* with you further in our upcoming meeting.

Regards,

Fred

Materials to remove barriers and prompt behaviours

It is important to make mapping your messages as easy as possible and reduce any excuses for not following through. Here are three key ideas to help with this:

1. Consider setting up email templates that follow the format. Emails of five lines or more offer an easy opportunity for practising the thinking strategies that underpin structuring your message. I include two example templates in the appendix, and provide 'cut and paste' versions in the Clarity Hub.

2. Create a folder, a SharePoint page or similar resource hub to house sample documents, links to tools offered in this book, templates and other resources. You may like to include links to the following (available inside the Clarity Hub):
   – my quick introductory video explaining how message maps work
   – the PowerPoint Planner, which guides you through each step of the message structuring process

3. Tailor templates to accommodate message maps. I cover melding message maps with corporate templates in chapter 6, but now is a good time to revisit and make sure the team is familiar with the relevant templates. You may like to add instructions using the language into the templates to help the team connect the dots between a message map and the template. I also provide an annotated example board paper template in my Clarity Hub.

Measurement to identify wins and areas for further focus

Like with any project, the only way to know if you are achieving your goals is to measure your progress. In this section, I run through several light-touch strategies to help you do that.

Set both effort and quality milestones and revisit them monthly during the first three months, and longer if warranted

Use effort milestones to be confident you will continue to use the approach regularly. For example, ensure:

▶ you have held or participated in briefing sessions for every paper going to a project steering committee, the senior leadership team or the board over the period

▶ your message map drafts are always peer reviewed before they are sent to leaders for review

▶ your emails of five lines or more apply message mapping principles (that is, a short introduction, one visible main message and a well-structured set of supporting points)

▶ you have used message maps to think through substantial contributions to meetings.

Use quality milestones to demonstrate that the effort is paying off. For example, ensure:

▶ your message maps are progressively receiving higher scores on the SCORE rubric

▶ your emails are of increasing quality and so leading to shorter 'chains', faster responses and less fire fighting

▶ stakeholders are making more comments about the quality of your communication.

You might even set yourself a challenge of receiving a compliment from a particularly surly stakeholder!

Self-evaluate and debrief regularly with your manager or buddy

You might do this fortnightly for the first month or two and monthly after that to maintain focus and calibrate progress.

Honesty combined with kindness will be key here. Give permission to yourself for real life and failure to get in the way of 'perfection'. If you are not comfortable admitting you are finding structuring your message difficult, or you have not consistently followed the principles over the recent period, you may pretend to yourself all is well even when you know it is not.

Listen to yourself and hold yourself accountable to not getting sloppy.

Keep track of the frequency that your manager reviews your communication

Ask yourself:

▶ Is my manager coming back to me with their suggestions more quickly than in the past?

▶ Am I continuing to reduce the amount of time my manager spends reviewing or rewriting my papers?

▶ If my manager needed to rewrite my paper, what caused this? Is this a one-off or systemic problem? If systemic, what can I do to further fine-tune our process to avoid a repeat?

Motivation to keep at it when the novelty wanes

Motivation is no small thing. As I have mentioned, a big part of improving your skills is simply doing it. Continuing to use the techniques will help you improve, even if there are times you pay less attention to quality than others. Here are four ideas to help.

Master the basics to be ruthlessly effective

At the time of writing I am reading Shane Parrish's new book, *Clear Thinking*. A footnote jumped out at me, so I share it here with you.

Here is what he said on page 27:

Most people are chasing complexity. They learn the basics enough to be average, then look for the secret, shortcut, or hidden knowledge.

Mastering the basics is the key to being ruthlessly effective. The basics might seem simple but doesn't mean they are simplistic.

The best in the world probably don't have some secret shortcut or hidden knowledge.

They merely understand the fundamentals better than others.

I don't think I need to add anything to this! Thinking skills can't be more fundamental, and this is what the Elevate framework is all about.

Helping you elevate the quality of thinking that you convey to your decision-makers (mostly!) during work hours too.

Use message maps when preparing for performance reviews

Performance reviews happen regularly in every organisation and so are a natural opportunity for practice at a time when team members are motivated to handle the meeting well. A message map will not only help you think through you situation, but also help you clarify your perspective on past performance and future ambitions.

This will give you a number of regular opportunities to consolidate your capability before baking your message into your day-to-day operating rhythm.

Focus ShowCases around message maps

ShowCases are baked into the Agile ways of working, and so may be familiar to you. If not, they are a simple idea that can help you too. Find an opportunity to share what you have achieved over the past quarter, if only to your manager.

Distilling down the key achievements provides an opportunity to practice while also raising the visibility of your substantive progress.

Make the most of your buddy

Helping a buddy with their communication helps you both, even if it does feel like work. Having opportunities to articulate what you have learned, sharing ideas on how to engage key stakeholders in your new approach and having someone to brag to is wonderful.

Depending on your personalities, you may even like to compete. How high did you score on the SCORE rubric for your last paper? How few alterations did your manager make on your last paper? How many compliments have you received on the lift in quality of your communication?

Don't be shy! Enjoy their successes as well as your own.

Thereafter: Make the new ways of working 'stick'

By now you will have made significant improvements to the clarity and quality of your communication. You should also be seeing a significant lift in velocity as you prepare better documents more quickly that support better, faster decision-making.

This is fantastic but also a risk as you may start to backslide as the novelty wears off. Here are five tactics to help you make the most of this approach.

1. *Update collateral:* Organisations routinely update templates and ways of working. Make sure to update templates. Add prompts to bake message structuring into new ways of working. If you have templates that are used company-wide, talk to your manager or leader about also updating those.

2. *Continue learning:* Message structuring is a skill that develops over time, with challenges emerging every time new stakeholders arrive and new roles are undertaken.

3. *Revisit concepts from this book:* Read a chapter and bring a takeaway to share at your next team meeting, along with an example of where that concept has helped you. Illustrate by sharing that example.

4. *Unscramble a message map:* Reconstructing a quality message map is a great way to practise your skills. If you have an old map you are proud of, cut it up and see if you can put it together again. I offer a number of these and other practical activities inside my Clarity Hub.

5. *Share your success:* I love hearing how people have used the ideas and encourage you to share your successes on our Engage Members area. You may also be inspired by those stories shared by others who have put these ideas into practice.

CHAPTER 9

Finish well

How many of the ideas in this book have you used now? My hope is many.

In fact, I hope you are not only doing things differently, but you are seeing different responses. Be that fewer clarification calls from email recipients, or less red pen from your manager ... either way, I hope you are feeling the progress.

If not, start now! Download the PowerPoint Planner[15] and take these steps to think through a piece of communication:

▶ Flush out your strategy, so you are confident you are communicating the right message to the right people.

▶ Frame your message using patterns as a quick start. This speeds you up, and also helps refine your thinking about your strategy and your message.

▶ Firm up your messaging using structured thinking techniques. These help you both work out what your messaging really is and also diagnose problems in your thinking.

▶ Finalise your document, making sure you visualise the hierarchy of your message so it's easy for your audience to find.

▶ Feed back and feed forward to make the most of each experience, helping you and your colleagues increase the value you deliver, time after time.

I wish you all the very best with your communication and leave you with one final thought.

Regardless of the format you need to convey your ideas in, it's the quality of your messaging that matters most.

---

15   ClarityFirstProgram.com/ClarityHub

APPENDIX

Appendix

▶ Core toolkit

▶ References and further reading

Elevate message mapping framework

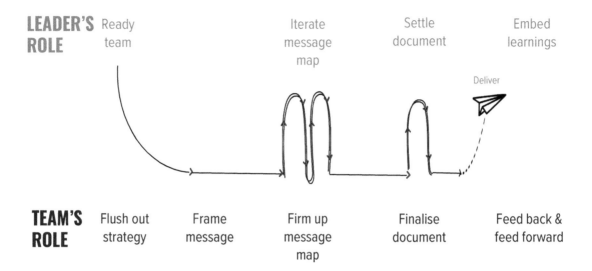

LEADER'S ROLE
Ready team · Iterate message map · Settle document · Embed learnings

Deliver

TEAM'S ROLE
Flush out strategy · Frame message · Firm up message map · Finalise document · Feed back & feed forward

Stakeholder analysis templates

#1 Clarify your purpose

As a result of this [email, paper, presentation, conversation], I want [my audience – name them] to [know, think, do ... what?]

#2 Understand your audience

Brainstorm the key players

#3 Map your stakeholders

Powerful influencers   *Decision-makers*

Degree of influence over the decision

Others   *Less powerful influencers*

Develop stakeholder strategy if key decision-makers are objectors

UNDERSTAND & SHIFT		What do they think now?	What do you want them to think?
	Objectors	Why don't they understand or agree?	
	Neutral	Why aren't they fully supportive?	

LEVERAGE		What do they support?	How much will they invest?	How could they help 'convert' your objectors?
	Champions	You? The concept? The goal?	Time? Money or other resources? Influence? Relationships?	Explain why they should support your idea?
				Ask them to meet so you can explain?
				Offer them a trade?
	Advocates			Help you revise your concept to make it more acceptable?
				Something else?

Pattern Picker framework

1 – CLARIFY OUTCOME	2 – REVIEW POTENTIAL MESSAGES	3 – FIND MESSAGE		4 – FIRM UP MESSAGE
I need my audience to ...	To achieve that I must explain ...	... then pick a pattern		... and structure it
> Action > Endorse > Implement > Support	Action plans How to proceed when persuasion not needed	Nike	Do X to fix Y	2–5 steps ordered by sequence or scale
> Know > Understand	Findings What was found when conducting analysis	Nugget	We found X	2–5 points of evidence ordered by scale of importance
> Trust	Updates That the status is green, project is going well	All is Well	We are in good shape	2–5 reasons why that is true, ordered by task or time
> Agree > Approve > Change > Decide > Endorse	Strategies How to capture an opportunity	Golden	Do X to capture opportunity	Opportunity exists, X will capture it, so do X
	How to solve a problem or capture an opportunity	Make the Case	Doing X will fix Y	2–5 reasons this is the right idea, e.g. strategy, returns, feasibility, risks
	How to solve a new problem	Oh Dear	Do X to solve problem	Problem exists, X will fix it, so do X
	Options Which options to evaluate	Short List	Consider these for solving Y	2–5 reasons to consider these options
	Best way to capture an opportunity or solve a problem	This or That	Option X is best for solving Y	These options may work, Option X is best, so do X
	Improvements How to tackle an emerging opportunity or risk	Change Tack	Change direction to reach goal	Have made progress, need to change direction to reach goal, so change direction
	How to succeed when you meet only some criteria	Step up	Do more to succeed at Y	Success requires X, we must do more to deliver X, so do more

Grouping structure summary

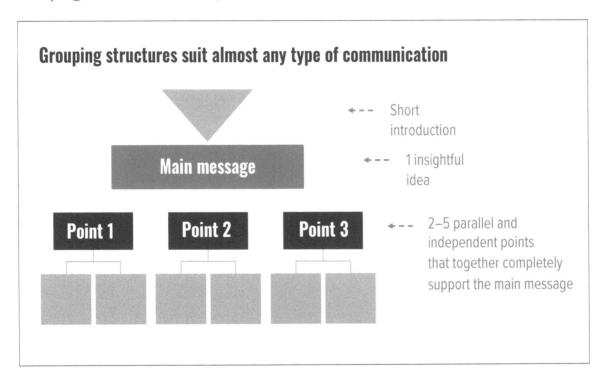

Grouping structures suit almost any type of communication

Main message

Point 1 Point 2 Point 3

Short introduction

1 insightful idea

2–5 parallel and independent points that together completely support the main message

Grouping structure with details

A short introduction that lets your audience know what you are discussing. It should include information that is familiar to the audience and bring their minds to a recent relevant event.

Most likely a single sentence that explains why you want to discuss the topic outlined above with your audience now.

The question you want to answer, which your audience will naturally want to ask after they have heard or read the context and trigger.

A single insightful message that is 25 words or less and summarises or ideally synthesises your whole story.

The single question your audience will naturally want to ask after learning your single message.

Point 1: The first of 2 to 5 points that respond to the same question your audience will naturally ask after hearing or reading the main message.	Point 2: The second of 2 to 5 points that responds to the same question the audience will naturally ask after hearing or reading the main message.	Points 3 to 5: More 'parallel' points if needed to further support the main message.
• The first of 2 to 5 sub-points that form either a grouping or deductive structure to elaborate on the top line point. • The second sub-point that follows the first, adopting either a grouping or deductive structure. • The third and subsequent sub-points, if necessary.	• As for point 1	• As for point 1

Deductive structure summary

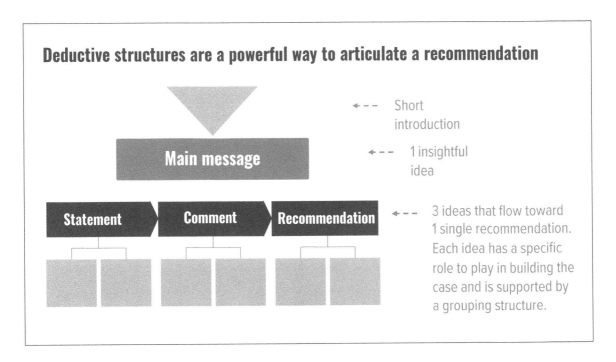

Deductive structure with details

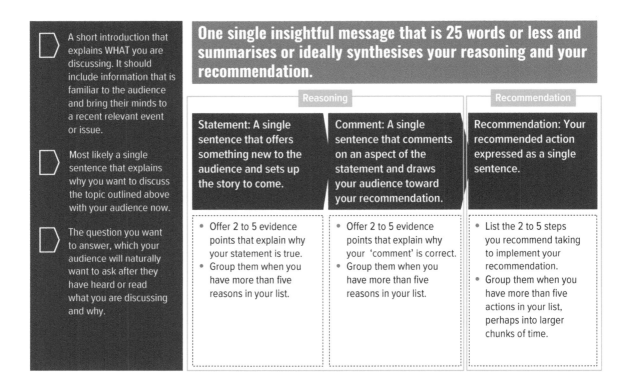

A short introduction that explains WHAT you are discussing. It should include information that is familiar to the audience and bring their minds to a recent relevant event or issue.

Most likely a single sentence that explains why you want to discuss the topic outlined above with your audience now.

The question you want to answer, which your audience will naturally want to ask after they have heard or read what you are discussing and why.

One single insightful message that is 25 words or less and summarises or ideally synthesises your reasoning and your recommendation.

Reasoning

Recommendation

Statement: A single sentence that offers something new to the audience and sets up the story to come.

Comment: A single sentence that comments on an aspect of the statement and draws your audience toward your recommendation.

Recommendation: Your recommended action expressed as a single sentence.

- Offer 2 to 5 evidence points that explain why your statement is true.
- Group them when you have more than five reasons in your list.

- Offer 2 to 5 evidence points that explain why your 'comment' is correct.
- Group them when you have more than five reasons in your list.

- List the 2 to 5 steps you recommend taking to implement your recommendation.
- Group them when you have more than five actions in your list, perhaps into larger chunks of time.

SCORE framework summary

**Sets the scene
quickly by drawing
the audience toward
one insightful
message**

What
Why
Main Message

**Conveys the right
balance of strategic
and operational
detail**

Strategy
Materiality

**Organises the ideas
in a well-structured
hierarchy**

Grouping
Deductive
MECE

**Readies the audience
for a productive
discussion**

Relevant
Readable

**Engages the audience
using a medium, style
and tone that suits
them**

Skimmable
Visual

SCORE framework – detailed

I ask whether the communication does the following Does it …

S – Set the scene quickly by drawing the audience toward one insightful message by:

1. Explaining **WHAT** is being discussed early, by ..
   a. Quickly reminding the audience about the familiar problem, opportunity or observation the paper will discuss
   b. Introducing that topic in a way that is timely and tight
2. Explaining **WHY** this topic is being discussed now
3. Offering **one insightful and visible main message** that unifies the whole paper in 25 words or less.

C – Convey the right balance of strategic and operational detail by:

4. Positioning the story appropriately in relation to strategy
5. Aligning with the right materiality thresholds for this audience

O – Organise the ideas in a well-structured hierarchy by:

6. Aligning ideas at every level of a grouping structure four ways:
   a. Number: Each group has two to five ideas
   b. Type: Each idea is the same kind of idea as its peers
   c. Vertically: Each idea answers the single natural question prompted by the idea above
   d. Horizontally: Ideas are arranged logically, likely by sequence or scale
7. Ensuring the top-line ideas in a deductive structure each play their specific role, ie
   a. The statement anchors the narrative around one substantive idea that is both new to the audience and broader in scope than the comment
   b. The comment narrows the discussion to focus on one key concept that was introduced in the statement
   c. The statement and comment are so persuasive that together they prepare your audience for your recommendation, so it does not come as a surprise

8. *Supporting the top-line of a deductive structure well, which means that*
   a. Both the statement and comment are supported by tightly grouped ideas
   b. The recommendation ('therefore') is supported by tightly grouped actions
9. *Avoiding gaps and overlaps, ie, the ideas are MECE (Mutually Exclusive, Collectively Exhaustive).* This involves:
   – Categorising and labeling ideas correctly
   – Avoiding ideas overlapping each other
   – Leaving nothing out

R – Readies the audience for a productive discussion by:

10. *Focusing only on matters relevant to the desired outcome*
11. *Being easily readable, using language that is active and parallel throughout, ie by*
   a. Synthesising or summarising ideas at every level into fully formed sentences that the audience will find insightful, ie useful, impactful and interesting
   b. Expressing ideas clearly, so the audience doesn't need to ask for clarification.
   c. Using parallel language so the ideas obviously match each other

E – Engages the audience using a medium, style and tone that suits them by:

12. *Formatting ideas so it is easy to skim the hierarchy of the messaging, in any medium*
13. *Using simple images, charts and diagrams to help the audience quickly grasp ideas*

Example message map

Recommendation:

Meeting regulatory requirements requires us to transition all 105 legacy reports into the case system by the end of this financial year. We have now reviewed the work plans and received updated estimates.

We are now ready to share those estimates with you along with potential ways forward.

What are you suggesting?

Decide whether to spend more or renegotiate requirements

We need to decide whether to spend $1.2 million to $2 million more over the coming two years or to renegotiate requirements with the regulator.

Despite stress testing all budgets, we can't transition all 105 regulatory reports within the agreed $2 million budget this financial year.	This means we need to decide which trade-offs to make as we work toward completing the 105 reports.	Therefore, we ask you to advise how we should proceed
Updated estimates for database came back at $2m, which is 2.5 x the original budget due to a more comprehensive holistic scoping. **Budgets for other aspects of the work have not materially changed.** • Workflow remains same. • API linking ditto. • Operational teams ditto. **Work required for reports identified since June last year has not been factored in.**	**We could spend $1.2m to $2m more over the coming two years.** • We could deliver everything in FY23 with $1.2m more during FY23, or • We could deliver some in FY23, some in FY24 with $2m or more in total. **We could renegotiate with the regulator.** • We could deliver only the top 70 reports by FY23 (fix existing 36, do another 35ish) within the current budget, or • We could seek agreement from the regulator to further extend the project and deliver all at a later date	**Decide whether to spend more …** • Decide whether to increase funding by $1.2m for FY23. • Decide whether to budget $2m more for the project in total and roll into next year. **Decide whether to renegotiate …** • Decide whether to accept the top 70 reports in FY23 as adequate. • Decide whether to seek extensions from the regulator.

RECOMMENDATION

The Regulatory Projects Steering Committee advises which trade-offs the team can make to finalise workplans for 2024.

EXECUTIVE SUMMARY

Meeting regulatory requirements requires us to transition all 105 legacy reports into the case system by the end of this financial year. We have now reviewed the plans and estimates and are ready to discuss potential ways forward.

In sum, we need to decide to either spend an extra $1.2 million to $2 million over the coming two years or renegotiate requirements with the regulator. Here is an outline of our high-level position before going into more detail below.

1. Despite stress testing all budgets, we can't transition all 105 regulatory reports within the agreed $2 million budget this financial year.
2. This means we need to make trade-offs when finalising the workplans.
3. As a result, we ask you to advise which trade-offs we can make.

DISCUSSION

Despite stress testing all budgets, we can't transition all 105 regulatory reports within the agreed $2 million budget this financial year. After conducting the thorough review that you requested, we found

- Updated estimates for database came back at $2 million – 2.5 times the original budget due to a more comprehensive scoping. (See appendix for breakdown.)
- Budgets for other aspects of the work have not materially changed. Costs for workflow, API linking, and operational aspects remain steady.
- Any reports that have been identified as needing to be reworked since June last year have not been factored into this.

This means we need to make trade-offs when finalising the workplans. Given these trade-offs require your endorsement to be implemented, we offer alternatives for your consideration.

Option 1: Spend $1.2 million more now or $2 million more later. We could then deliver either

- everything in FY23 with $1.2 million more during FY23
- some in FY23, some in FY24 with $2 million or more.

Option 2: Renegotiate scope or time with the regulator. If taking this path, we could

- limit the scope to delivering only the top 70 reports by FY23 within the current budget and negotiate with the regulator to accept this as final, or
- seek agreement from the regulator to further extend project timelines.

As a result, we ask you to advise which trade-offs we can make. This involves deciding whether to

- Spend more by either
  - increasing funding by $1.2 million for FY23, or
  - budgeting $2 million more for the project in total and roll into next year.
- Renegotiate by either
  - accepting the top 70 reports in FY23 as adequate and convincing the regulator to agree, or
  - seeking extensions from the regulator.

We understand this is not the outcome you were hoping for but look forward to your decision as to the best way forward.

ATTACHMENTS

Detailed financial breakdown of the updated financial estimates for all aspects of the 105 reports project.

SUBMITTED BY

Ryan Bloggs, Program Manager, Regulatory Projects

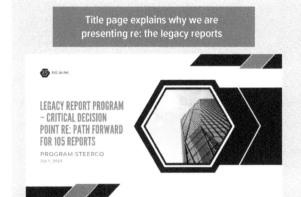

Meeting regulatory requirements requires us to transition all 105 legacy reports into the case system by the end of this financial year.

We have now reviewed plans and estimates and are ready to discuss potential ways forward.

We need to decide to either spend $1.2 million to $2 million more over the coming two years or to renegotiate requirements with the regulator

Despite stress-testing all budgets, we can't transition all 105 regulatory reports within the agreed $2 million budget this financial year

01 — Updated estimates for database came back at $2m, which is 2.5 x the original budget due to a more comprehensive scoping. (See appendix for breakdown.)

02 — Budgets for other aspects of the work have not materially changed. Costs for workflow, API linking, and operational aspects remain steady.

03 — Work required for reports identified since June last year has not been factored in.

We need to decide which tradeoffs to make so we can finalise our work plans for completing the 105 reports

We ask you to advise which tradeoffs we can make in rescoping the project

We need to decide whether we

Spend more by
1. increasing funding by $1.2m for FY23
2. budgeting $2m more for the project in total and roll into next year.

Renegotiate by
1. accepting the top 70 reports in FY23 as adequate and convincing the regulator to agree
2. seeking extensions from the regulator.

Email templates

Pre-formatted email signatures

These are available for download in the Clarity Hub, or alternatively you can copy type them from here.

Email signature idea #1

Hello xxx …

['WHAT': Introduce the topic you wish to discuss in a way that is relevant right now]

['WHY': Explain why you wish to discuss this topic in this email]

[MAIN MESSAGE – Articulate a single, powerful and overarching message in 25 words or less]

- [Support 1]
- [Support 2]
- [Support 3 – if needed]
- [Support 4 – if needed]
- [Support 5 – if needed]

I hope that helps.

Cheers,

Dav

Email signature idea #2

Hello xxx …

Using a visual layout helps both you and your audience to see the hierarchy of your messaging. This template is here to remind you how to do that.

In short, use formatting to signal which part of the structure each element belongs to. In more detail:

- Make the main message pop off the page using white space and bold.
- Use bullets and/or numbers to encourage you to break out your points and avoid 'block shock'.
- Break up sections that are longer than three lines so your audience can find your point without working too hard.

I hope that helps.

Cheers,

Dav

I have included a copy of this in the Clarity Hub Toolkit. Equally, you could copy it from here.

Hi colleague/boss,

I have been thinking about *X* issue and have outlined my early thinking on a page for your consideration.

Before you review it, I'd like to explain how the page works so the diagram makes sense to you.

1. **It is a discussion draft.** Although the ideas are, I hope, in a clear and logical place within the structure, the ideas are very much open for debate.

2. **The draft outlines my current thinking in a way that may seem more direct than usual.** You will see that the ideas are anchored around a single message that is crafted as a point of view. The technique I am using flushes out the main thought up-front, before diving into the details.

3. **Once we agree on the messaging, we can turn these ideas into a well-structured document.** I would like to hold off on preparing the document until we agree on the ideas to minimise rework. Focusing on the one-pager first will keep us focused on the main ideas and encourage us to 'nail these' without being distracted by document formatting. My experience so far suggests we can save time this way.

I look forward to discussing issue *X* with you further in our upcoming meeting.

Regards,

Fred

References and further reading

Books

Aristotle (~4th century BC), *Rhetoric*

Bryar, C & Carr, B (2021), *Working Backwards*, St. Martin's Press

Drucker, P (2013), *People and Performance*, Harvard Business Review Press

Grant, A (2021), *Think Again*, Viking

Hyatt, M (2019), *Free to Focus*, Baker Publishing Group

Johnson, W (2022), *Smart Growth: How to Grow Your People to Grow Your Company*, Harvard Business Review Press

Kolko, J (2010), 'Abductive thinking and sensemaking: The drivers of design synthesis', *Design Issues*

Lombardo, M & Eichinger, R (2010), *The Career Architect Development Planner*, Lominger

McKeon, G (2021), *Effortless*, Currency

Medcalf, R (2022), *Making Time for Strategy*, Xquadrant

Minto, B (2021), *The Minto Pyramid Principle*, Pearson Education Limited

Minto, W (2018), *Logic, Inductive and Deductive*, Franklin Classics

Moore, MG (2021), *No Bullshit Leadership*, Rosetta Books

Newport, C (2016), *Deep Work*, Grand Central Publishing

Pink, D (2005), *A Whole New Mind*, Riverhead Books

Soojung-Kim Pang, A (2020), *Shorter*, Penguin General UK

Stanley, D & Castles, G (2017), *The So What Strategy*, Clarity Know How

Varol, O (2020), *Think like a Rocket Scientist*, WH Allen

Watson, D (2004), *Watson's Dictionary of Weasel Words*, Vintage Australia

Zelazny, G (2001), *Say it with Charts*, McGraw Hill

Zelazny, G (2006), *Say it with Presentations*, McGraw Hill

Tools and Downloads

Clarity Hub - ClarityFirstProgram.com/ClarityHub (first month free)

Email course - ClarityFirstProgram.com/Emails (free)

▶ About the author

Davina is the founder of Clarity First. She blends her education and consulting experience to design and deliver innovative and engaging programs for clients globally.

Davina began her communication coaching career at McKinsey & Company in Hong Kong. She worked for the Firm in a mix of full-time and freelance communication roles for around 18 years. This involved helping consultants improve their communication, designing and facilitating learning programs in individual offices and for Firm Learning as well as supporting the Asia Pacific Marketing Practice.

Since then, she has built an international stable of predominantly tech, retail and finance clients. This involves helping leaders set up their teams to prepare papers and presentations that those same leaders no longer need to rewrite.

Davina lives in Seattle, Washington with her husband. She loves spending time with her two adult sons and broader family in Australia and the UK.

Learn more about her work at ClarityFirstProgram.com

Printed in Australia
Ingram Content Group Australia Pty Ltd
AUHW010903250724
397511AU00001B/1